Deep in the Green

DEEP IN THE GREEN

An Exploration of Country Pleasures

Anne Raver

Alfred A. Knopf NEW YORK 1995

All of the articles in this work were originally published in
The New York Times, copyright © 1992, 1993, 1994
by The New York Times Company, and in *Newsday*,
copyright © 1985, 1986, 1987, 1988, 1989, 1990, 1991 by
Newsday, Inc., and are reprinted here by permission.

Library of Congress Cataloging-in-Publication Data
Raver, Anne.
Deep in the green : an exploration of country pleasures /
Anne Raver. — 1st ed.
p. cm.
ISBN 0-679-43483-6
1. Gardening—Long Island—New York. 2. Country life—Long
Island—New York. 3. Raver, Anne. I. Title.
SB455.R34 1995
635'.09747'21—dc20 95-15718
CIP

Manufactured in the United States of America

First Edition

To Kathleen, Ginger and Molly

Contents

Contents

Contents

Introduction

*T*he best part about writing about the garden is that it's so big. You can write about love, as sphinx moths visit the evening primroses opening up at dusk and bats swoop in to sip nectar from the saguaro cactus. You can write about death as the soldier bug prongs a Mexican bean beetle lunching on a leaf—or your own father's failing heart, as the Japanese beetles move in to devour his rosebushes. You can write about beloved pets who ride to Agway with you, and eat half your ice cream cone. And who die, halfway through your own life, so you have to go it alone.

And when you get tired of writing about life and death in the garden, and whether or not the sprinkler that goes "swish-swish-swish" works better than the one that goes "thump-thump-thump, eh-eh-eh," you can travel to greater gardens, like Yellowstone, where I saw the emerald green grass spring up out of the ashes of the fires of 1988, or the Amazon, where I talked to folk healers and farmers who planted by the cycles of the river, and followed botanists through the rain forest as they collected plants in a buggy jungle that not only may hold the cure for AIDS or cancer, but also are the basis of daily medicine—for bronchitis, diarrhea, hemorrhaging after labor—for millions of people. I have gotten up before dawn with drought-stricken farmers in Missouri, and shivered in a duck blind in Nebraska waiting for the cranes to come back to the Platte River in March.

This book isn't so much about gardening as it is about making connections—to all the plants and creatures that populate the earth. It's about noticing things, from the fish in a neighbor's pond lying belly up after some pesticide truck sprayed the trees, to a line of lifeless sycamores on a street that was showered with salt to melt the ice of an endless winter.

It's about the joy of obsession. Of gardeners who speak in loving tones to giant squashes and melons, and demand that their newspaper's garden columnist ride from one end of the kingdom to the other to identify some mysterious weed. It's about friends—who drive hundreds of miles to pull weeds and dig up bushes on the old family farm, and joyfully take over the kitchen to bake pies and make pesto and sit around the table drinking wine long after a proper farmer would be in bed.

This is not a book that will tell you how to site your garden, or which of the old roses you dare not live without. It does not unravel the mysteries of science or even the Linnaean binomial system. It tells the story of the earthworm and the sea turtle. Of a goose separated from her goslings on the Long Island Expressway. Of the children of farmers who now live in big cities—as the old fields turn into house lots and golf courses. It's about growing old. It's about losing things you love. Dogs, places, people.

But as any gardener knows, it is about going on. Building new gardens, if the old one has been ravaged by a hurricane—or a housing development. Taking the spirit of a beloved dog or person with you, long after you have buried her, as you take a walk she would have loved, or bake his favorite pie, or set the bright faces of Autumn Beauty sunflowers in a lovely old vase from your mother's house.

Deep in the Green

Pulling Up Roots

I didn't plant my snap peas this year. I'm moving to Long Island—to a warmer, sandier soil—and someone else will be tilling my old plot in Ipswich, Massachusetts.

It's a beautiful site for a garden, a fifty-foot square in the middle of a wild meadow. It basks in full sunlight on the top of a knoll overlooking the confluence of the Ipswich River and a saltwater creek. At low tide, I can lean on my shovel and watch the clam diggers and the great blue herons; at high tide, the more frivolous boaters, speeding down the channel like Toady and Rat.

Leaving a piece of land is not an easy departure. Each place holds so many experiences—successes and failures with plants, bugs and people—that a move can't help feeling like some kind of erasure.

My husband and I first hacked at the matted field with borrowed pickaxes, ripping up the sod with our hands and shaking the topsoil from every piece back into the little square we had bounded by twine. He, a suburban kid, thought a small plot was plenty; I, a farmer's daughter, wanted half the field—for squash, potatoes and corn.

Months before, we'd argued over the seed catalogs. Why couldn't I be satisfied with a tidy little list, he grumbled. That was just like me, always wanting too much. Why couldn't I plant corn if I wanted, I complained. That was just like him, always trying to control me. You want to do everything *your way*, we both yelled, like furious adolescents.

Neither of us had learned the art of compromise, and as we went down the rows planting the beans and putting in the tomatoes, our boundaries solidified into rock walls, instead of blending in a comfortable combination of desires and tastes. When a pound of Burpee's Early Sunglow arrived in the mail—I'd willfully, secretly added it to the list—my husband turned on our big color TV and began rooting for the Red Sox. After all, maybe his favorite vegetation was the bright green outfield of Fenway Park.

The next April, I knelt in the cold damp earth, putting in as many peas as I wanted. My husband and I had given up on gardening together—and on each other. The first little green shoots comforted me, in their sturdy urgency to get on with life, but the irony of my huge plot, for just me, was a bitter one. Who was going to eat all those vegetables that would fill the hefty Sears freezer my father had bought for us?

I began to grow flowers that summer. I realized why my father puttered in his rose beds, his own heart opening up as the hybrid teas and grandifloras bloomed. And by the time other men ventured into my garden, I knew enough to hand them the packet of Kentucky Wonder seeds and say, with a nonchalant shrug, "Plant them however you want, that's part

of the fun." Sure, I was gritting my teeth, but I wanted to eat those beans across from a warm body.

Yet that little seaside plot also gave me clarity, helped me to trust my instincts. I longed for rhubarb, raspberries and asparagus, but I couldn't bring myself to put in any of these perennials with any of my gardening guests.

Perhaps I needed to do it all my own way for a while. I'd grown up with a man who'd welcomed his children in the vegetable plot—as long as we set the tomatoes out with military precision. No wonder my own garden grew in crooked rows and irregular patches, a slightly sloppy riot of vegetables and flowers. A kind of happy manifestation of my mind, which is more circular than linear.

But last summer, some blight seemed to pass through my healthy plot. The soil wasn't the problem; it had grown rich with years of compost and my neighbor's cow manure. It wasn't ignorance; I knew how to combat every bug and fungus. No, some malaise of my own had crept up to that seaside garden. When the Japanese beetles arrived, I failed to pick them off the bush beans in the evenings. I no longer stood patiently with the hose, letting my thirsty tomatoes drink their fill. Days would pass, and I'd stay away—playing with friends or reading wintry books inside the house—and when I did climb to the top of my little knoll, I'd find weeds choking my cucumbers, spider mites smothering my Brussels sprouts. It was no longer a happy experience to grow all this stuff alone. My little paradise had become a Garden of Neglect.

And so last fall, as I brought in the green tomatoes, and cut off the drooping heads of my Mammoth sunflowers, I knew that the spring would send me out into some new territory. I don't know what my new garden will be like. Some small suburban plot, set right against my neighbor's private hedge? Or a more private place, tucked behind the cottage on some wealthy old estate?

I'll miss the sea, and the herons, and the deer stepping delicately out into the meadow as the sun goes down. But I know that my next garden will put down longer, woodier roots. I find myself reading up on those asparagus beds. I'm studying the art of orchards. And I want my own grape arbor—to make enough wine for two.

Putting Down Roots

When I saw the cottage, my heart said, Take it, you belong here. But my father's practical voice cautioned: Why fall in love with a place you can only rent? You should buy, get a tax write-off.

But look at it, I told the father in me. An old red cottage with a screened-in porch sat a stone's throw from a salt marsh where great blue herons waded at low tide and black ducks paddled among the weeds. A wild garden full of jewel-weed and lady's thumb spilled over the old barnyard of a tumbledown stable, rambler roses and raspberry bushes covered the log fence that bordered the house. Crows cawed from the bare branches of a tall black walnut. A swing hung from a sugar maple, in silent invitation.

All this, the unconscious mind understood in a moment. Before the conscious mind, the critic, the linear thinker that gets us from point A to point B, the self that makes us believe that life is a matter of putting one foot in front of the other, said, Too much rent, better buy. All this beauty is beside the point.

Inside the cottage were a kitchen just made for cooking soup, baking bread; a nook surrounded by windows, perfect for a dining room table; a sunny living room turning gold from the marsh; and upstairs, two sweet gabled rooms. A full moon would shine right in on the pillow.

But I said to the owner, "I guess not. If I move out of Brooklyn, it'll be to buy a place. You know. Stop throwing money down the rent hole. Make an investment. Get some of that tax money back." Besides, it's too isolated in the country. There are so many more interesting events and people, for a single woman, in the city.

The owner of the cottage looked surprised. His old shoes were muddy from the flats we'd just walked through, talking of canoeing at high tide, and that little brown shack across the river, where you can buy lobsters, cheap. But he shrugged politely, a tribute to his breeding. Well, then. That's that, his shoulders said, and like the sun dipping behind the trees, all the meaning drained out of our conversation.

This wasn't just a case of a man trying to get money for a house. It was more that I'd just suggested how beautiful climbing hydrangea would look, winding itself up the trees around his house; just told him how the English train clematis to weave itself among the roses. And then, like a woman trifling with a man's feelings, I said, On second thought, I can't do it, and it felt cold on the marsh.

The next day, I wandered about the office in a fog, feeling like a child who'd been betrayed. Only it was I, of course, who'd betrayed myself.

I'd moved to Brooklyn, from Long Island, last spring, to

escape the malls, the tract developments, the insulated lives of my rich neighbors. And it was a relief to walk past grand-mothers on their stoops, to buy crusty bread a block from my home, to see a black or Asian face without registering it as an event. But all this culture I'd intended to enjoy—museums, galleries, poetry readings, bookstores—was a pipe dream that suffered a slow death on the exhausting two-to-three-hour daily commute from home to office and back again.

And the bad air was getting to me. And the noise, coming from all sides: the kids on the street, the quarreling next door, the stereo upstairs, the F train rumbling below. I loved Prospect Park and its elegant old trees, but sit under one af-ter dark and you're dead.

This isn't paranoia, it's being streetwise. In the city, you live with a certain low-level fight-or-flight response that's so ready to turn on, it feels as if it never turns off, and such constant readiness is a drain on your electrical system. Af-ter a while, you don't really notice it, but you feel tired all the time.

It's disturbing, on an existential level, to question if you re-ally should sleep with a window open, on a summer's night, or walk the ten blocks home, rather than take a cab. Every cautionary act is a little closing of the prison gate, but that's what the Central Park jogger said to herself when she de-cided she wasn't going to stop running after dark.

Not that people don't get murdered outside the city. Or that there's no child abuse or drug addiction. Or husbands who kill their wives. Or homeless people wheeling their shopping carts down New York Avenue in Huntington. It's just a matter of numbers and space, and money. The violence out in the suburbs is a little more hidden, like the backyards.

And as you travel east, the backyards lose their hedges and merge with fields and woods and tidal estuaries.

I didn't think about all these things the day after I'd said no to the cottage on the river. I just wandered about the office, feeling lost. Until I talked to a friend, and realized, in describing the place, how much I wanted it. When I have one foot in the grave, will I kick myself for losing a few tax benefits? I called the owner and got no answer, and spent a long, anxious evening dialing his number. Finally, he answered.

"I've changed my mind," I said. "I was trying to be practical. But I really want to live there."

"Well," he said. "There's nothing more practical than living in a place you love."

And so, on one of the rainiest days of the year, and the worst traffic jams on the Brooklyn-Queens Expressway, I moved from Brooklyn, back to Long Island, to a wilder, quieter Island than the one I'd known before. My dog, Molly, in the front seat. My cat, Mrs. Grey, under the rubber plant. Packed in with garden books, computer, espresso pot, unanswered letters, unread *New Yorkers*, an herb garden, two clematis vines. Followed by a moving van with Grandmother's rocking chair, old furniture from the family farm, boxes of books and files, a futon that marked my hippie days, a mattress and box spring marking middle age. Whiskey barrels and a cold frame. More plants from the garden. What, the men said. You want us to move the tree that grows in Brooklyn?

It's wrenching to move, even to a place that feels more like home. To leave the Polish lady next door, and the old man who sits on the stoop, and the shy deli owner who always insists on putting everything, even one little item, in a plastic bag. As you get older, every attachment gains importance. There isn't time to keep making new ones.

"Why are you so afraid to put down roots?" my friend Joe said to me a couple months ago. "You're like a piece of plankton floating around in the bay. And nothing can attach itself to you." It was Joe who showed me the cottage, figuring I could put down roots by a river. Even if it's just renting. When you love a place, things develop.

The first night in my cottage, I thought the lack of noise was deafening: no stereo, no arguing voices, no rumbling trains. An owl kept me awake. And my own vibrations, tuning in to night noises in the cottage, on the marsh.

It's important to have a sense of place. To feel that you belong somewhere, to feel committed. For some people, place begins with another person, and everything—from friends to the Japanese maple in the yard—grows from that. But sometimes, it works the other way. You find a place where you belong. And the people find you. Gathering mussels, picking beans, eating blackberry pie.

Breaking the Mold

$\mathcal{M}$y friendly local entomologist, Gary Couch, stuck a pin in my "beneficial bugs" fantasy this spring.

I'd already filled out my Burpee's order: a half pint of ladybugs ($9.95), a carton of praying mantis eggs ($4.95), a package of Trichogramma wasps ($4.25) and two Bag-A-Bug Japanese beetle traps ($9.95 each).

I could just see those cute little red ladybugs patrolling for aphids, mealybugs, leafhoppers, flea beetles. My praying mantises—who've always reminded me of nearsighted professors—saying daily grace over their dinners of beetles, cabbage loopers, the hated cutworm.

Couch snickered. "Riii-ght. Like the ad for praying mantises I saw from one of the seed catalogs: *'More ferocious than tigers!'*"

He dropped a dried-up-looking vine borer moth into a little glass jar. "Well, it's true," he conceded. "Even tigers don't devour their own young." Then he gave me a little impromptu bug lecture:

When those mail-order praying mantises hatch out of their egg cases, they're going to be ravenous. And the first thing they'll lay eyes on is each other. So though you may start out with a hundred little green mantises, in about an hour, you'll find yourself with *one* very full survivor of the fittest.

And another thing: The praying mantis is an indiscriminate eater. It'll just as soon munch on a nice honeybee as a loathsome beetle, and it won't stop there. It'll move out of the insect world—on to salamanders, little shrews, even the beneficial frog! (I like frogs so much I've built little coffee-can huts for them and made drinking troughs from peanut butter lids.) As Couch prattled on, I began to wonder if my dog, Molly, would be safe. She's about the size of a small heifer and she likes to wander at night. Just how big could a well-fed praying mantis get?

I crossed praying mantises off my list.

Then Couch turned to ladybugs. I'd been thinking of them as tiny decorative pets, hopping happily about my bean plants, sunning themselves on broad, healthy leaves until some mealybug made an appearance. Forget it, said Couch. You need a regular plague to keep an army of ladybugs around. And after gorging themselves on an infestation of aphids, these eat-and-run types will move on—and out of your garden.

For most of these mail-order bugs, said Couch, timing is everything. Suppose those mealybugs don't arrive until the week after the postman brings your box of ladybugs? Do you think they'll stick around and wait a week? Fat chance. They'll be in Idaho by then—headed back home for California.

"Most of the ladybugs advertised in seed catalogs are a California species," said Couch. "In the fall, they fly up from the agricultural valleys to hibernate in the mountain canyons, and that's where the insectaries collect them—scooping them up by the thousands and putting them in buckets."

So when you let your ladybugs loose in the garden, they're just waking up from a long winter's nap. They see it's spring and figure it's time to fly back home—to their California valleys.

"It's a dormancy habit that's hard to break," said Couch.

I crossed ladybugs off the list. That left wasps and Bag-A-Bug traps. But Couch wouldn't lay off. For years I've watched the Trichogramma wasp lay her white eggs on the backs of my tomato hornworms (those bright green ridged monsters with little horns on their heads and suction cups for feet), each wasp egg sounding another death knell for my favorite enemy. Once those white eggs showed up on the worms' backs, I'd forgo my favorite method of pest control—jumping on the rubbery creeps with my Nikes, stabbing them viciously with my trowel. I could sit back and cooperate with nature.

Heh-heh, said Couch. "The trouble with the wasp is it doesn't kill the hornworm until its feeding stage is over—because it's getting nourished from the larva. And by then, most of the damage is done."

As for those other wasps that are getting all the hype this year—*Pediobius foveolatus*—they may eat up your Mexican bean beetles, *if* you get the timing right. The baby wasps like to feast on the insides of the beetle larvae, but if the two life cycles aren't exactly matched, you've sunk your money into an organic fantasy.

Couch gave me two aspirin. He tried to comfort me with

his favorite subject—encouraging good local bugs to stick around by planting their favorite foods near the garden. Making gizmos out of aluminum foil and bright yellow paint to confuse the bugs, with their tiny little brains.

He unfolded a large piece of cardboard covered with foil. "I put this underneath my cabbage plant, and the mother aphid flies in looking for a place to lay her eggs. Now the only way she can tell up from down is by the difference in color between the ground and the sky. . . ." He quirked his eyebrows at me. Yeah, yeah, I got it. The aluminum foil reflects the blue sky and suddenly that dumb little aphid finds herself flying upside down. . . .

Very clever, but I'd had enough for one day. I went home with the Bag-A-Bugs still on my list. Couch said they were okay—as long as I put them up twenty-five feet outside the garden.

There was that trace of a snicker again. "You want to lure them *away* from your beans, not toward them," he reminded me.

I wandered aimlessly about the house until the phone rang. It was Dad, bragging about his spinach crop. Not a cutworm in miles. Doused the whole garden in Diazinon this year. I stared out the window facing my own little plot. I come from a long line of pesticide users. And like the ladybug flying back to California, I almost ran down to the hardware store—for a little chemical poison.

Up with Peas

There are some things in life that give me great comfort, and one of them is planting peas.

I'd had a difficult week, the kind that makes the future look gloomy, and the voices start chipping away: Things will never change. You're doing it again. You're going to grow old like this. You, your dog and your cat. Only they'll die first.

Not the kind of mood, in short, that sends you skipping down the garden path with your hoe. But gardeners have a clock in their heads that tends to override these occasional bouts of grief, these what-does-it-all-mean little moods.

This clock has no face or friendly little tick-tick-tick. No lighted green numbers. It's more like planets in orbit, a huge contraption, something Leonardo da Vinci might have designed. Or maybe it was made at Stonehenge, after the first wheel was invented. Because this clock is older than time; it's like a big stone rolling through the seasons, and we mortal gardeners, whether we're in the mood or not, find ourselves obeying it.

Maybe this clock is just the sun, which rises earlier every day. This morning it was a rippling strip of gold on the bay. And it was saying, peas, peas, peas. Spinach, spinach, spinach. Shallots, shallots, shallots. It should have said shallots a week ago, but it's an old clock, after all.

Anyway, I went down to the garden with my Burpee Sugar Daddies and Snappies, which I'd soaked overnight, to hasten germination, and my little bag of legume inoculant.

The legume inoculant is nitrogen-fixing bacteria, and if you dust your damp peas with the stuff, you'll be sure to get things off to a good start.

The reason you need the bacteria has to do with this wonderful quality peas share with all legumes. This family is like those perfect houseguests—who always leave gifts after their stay. Peas are able to pull nitrogen out of the air and turn it into food. Not like greedy corn, for instance, which pulls nitrogen from the soil—and leaves nothing behind.

The pea is civilized. It evolved in poor soil—so it had to take nitrogen where it could get it: the air. Then it struck an agreement with tiny bacteria called rhizobia, which formed nodules on the roots, and helped them take phosphorus from the soil, a necessity for turning atmospheric nitrogen into food. The rhizobia, lucky for us, also happen to leave nitrogen in the surrounding soil. Which is why I always invite the pea plant back every spring. And sometimes I'll plant them where the corn, the slobovian houseguest, last ate me out of house and home. Just to put some nitrogen back in the cupboard.

But even if peas ate everything I had, I'd still plant them. I'd dump truckloads of aged manure on them, if that's what it took to grow those crispy, sweet snap peas. Sugar Daddies in seventy-four days. Snappies in sixty-three days.

But I wasn't really thinking of my stomach the other day. I was enjoying the mythic comfort of turning over the sandy earth, and feeling the sun on my back. It was a mild, cloudy day, the kind that keeps you thinking: Oops, there's the sun, I think I'll take my sweater off. Oops, it's turned gray all of a sudden, kind of chilly now, better put my sweater back on. But I didn't mind. It was yet another spring ritual. And besides, nature was cooperating. The weatherman had announced a 40 percent chance of rain, but so far, I was enjoying the 60 percent.

I got down on my hands and knees, and went at the earth with what I call the claw—a hand cultivator with three prongs. I'd decided to plant my peas in last year's squash patch, which happens to back up against a crumbling concrete wall that faces south and warms the soil at its feet.

Peas like cool weather. The seeds germinate when the soil reaches 40 degrees, and this soil felt about right, though I didn't feel like getting all scientific with a soil thermometer. I suppose this is a failing in a garden writer—I'm *supposed* to perform these neat little experiments and report the results— but doing so spoils what I love about gardening. The way your mind wanders as you pull yet another rock the size of an ostrich egg out of a spot that last fall was as finely tilled as pastry flour. What goes on down there in the winter, I always wonder. Maybe I'll tell you next week.

My spirits started to lift. The dim sunshine lay gently on the bare trees and the pink leaf buds of the wild roses. Molly, my collie mutt, took up her usual position at the top of the hill, where she watches for the mailwoman, who tosses dog treats from her window.

I made my trench four inches deep and six inches wide, just as I first learned from the late James Crockett. There may be better techniques, ways that have been discovered since his death, but this is my annual spring tip of the cap to one of the world's fine gardeners. I found a little cutworm and thought for a split second of the Buddhists' reverence for all living things. Then I squished it. I took off my gloves, to feel the soil between my fingers, and tossed out the last few pebbles.

Then I poured the peas into an old clean coffee can and sprinkled some inoculant on them, tossing them about until they were lightly covered. You only need to do this once for a new pea plot, by the way, because rhizobia live for years in the soil. Then I placed the peas, an inch apart, all over the trench, covered them with an inch or so of soil, and tamped the whole row down. As the peas grow, I'll pull soil in from the sides of the trench to keep the roots cool, just as Crockett advised. And I'll be careful not to step on the row and compact the soil—because what peas need most for nitrogen fixation is oxygen, and if air is squeezed out of the ground, they won't do so well.

The row is wide, and I'll put my fence—a six-footer of sturdy tomato wire—right down the middle, so the vines can scramble up either side. You have to sink those fence posts deep because the weight of a good crop of fat Snappies can pull the whole thing down in a good wind. And I like tomato wire better than netting because it has big squares—essential for grabbing fistfuls of sweet crunchy peas at grazing time.

I leaned on my shovel, and noticed one last patch of snow on the shady side of the garden. But a cheerful green color was also showing beneath the plastic cover of my cold frame. This was stuff I'd given up for dead after a January freeze. But here it was, spinach, corn salad, lettuce, looking almost salad-bowl-size. I mixed up some fish emulsion and gave the greens a little pep-up drink. I planted a new row of my favorite Melody spinach. I found myself humming a silly little song from my childhood, feeling okay.

That's what planting peas in winter will do for you. You go out to the garden with a chill in your heart, and spring warms it right up.

The Poop on Crickets

I got four pounds of cricket manure down in Georgia from a guy holding a Beefmaster tomato that looked like the Elephant Man.

"This big ole monster here weighs two pound, ten ounces," said Bill Bricker. "It's ugg-ly, but it has resistance to disease, and it's de-licious."

His lime green farmer's hat said Bricker's Organic Farm, but calling Bill Bricker a farmer is sort of like calling Hunter Thompson a minister. The man was handing me a little bag of sure-as-you're-born cricket manure.

"It takes four hundred . . ." He paused here, to let it sink in. "Four hundred and twenty-five thousand cc's—you know what cc's are, doncha?"

No, sir, I don't.

"Cricket crap," he said, a grin on his face.

"It takes"—you gotta be patient in the South—"four hundred and twenty-five thousand cc's to make four pounds of Gotta Grow."

I'd seen a lot of garden products that day—garden writers' conferences attract more of 'em than whiteflies to a yellow sticky trap—but this was intriguing.

"Twice as rich as chicken manure," Bricker was saying, hefting the Elephant Man tomato.

Come on, now. Richer than la crème de la crème?

"Nitrogen content, four-*point*-six-nine," he said. "Phosphorus, three-point-*O*-seven, and po-tash, two. Plenty of calcium. Roses go bananas."

Then Bricker launched into a life that sounds like it just sort of sprung up, like a tomato growing out of a compost pile.

"I've been making compost for about twenty-five years, since I was at Leavenworth, and I don't mean the penitentiary," he said. "I'm talking about command school, where they brainwash ya for the Pentagon."

Bricker lived in one of those little army boxes on the edge of an endless Kansas prairie, so he dug up a speck of it for a garden—and started building a compost pile.

"Leaves, grass clippings, manure. Something green and something brown is all you need. Lo and behold, the next spring, a tomato came up," he said. "It grew and it grew and I fertilized it, and pretty soon, it covered the whole pile. I don't know how many tomatoes it bore, but the three boys and the wife, and all the neighbors ate off it, and I got one wheelbarrow load off it when wintertime came. We ate 'em up to Christmas."

You know how the army is. They send you here, they send you there. Vietnam. Ohio.

"I learned Thai no trouble, but I never did figure out what

language they were speaking in Cleveland," said Bricker. When he got assigned to Newark, New Jersey, he decided he didn't want to learn any more foreign languages. He retired early, to Augusta, to do what he loved. Composting.

Bricker sells topsoil, rich with silt from the Savannah River bottom, organic potting soil, soilless mix and "Compostost, Breakfast for Flowers." Compostost is a mix of manure, blood meal, granite meal and wood fiber that is, well, like Wheaties for plants. Bricker's always looking for new products, and when he heard about Ghann's Cricket Farm, just a hop across town, he smelled a winner.

"They sell a lot of crickets around here for fish bait, and this is a European hybrid that gets fed fish meal and soybean meal and ground corn and molasses," said Bricker. "Guaranteed twenty-five percent pro-tein—so they're eating better than you or I, Sugar."

Local farmers had been trucking manure in and out of Ghann's Cricket Farm for years. Spreading it on their tomato fields, growing gigundo peppers and cukes. So Bricker went over and got himself some. Planted three test plots. One with cricket manure, one with his own favorite compost and one with plain old 10-10-10.

"I got giants out of all three, but the difference was the taste," said Bricker. "There's something about manure—cricket or otherwise—that makes a tomato sweet."

Then Bricker discovered a wonderful thing. He mixed up a little cc-tea—a cup to five gallons of water—and poured it down the middle of his compost pile, to speed up the decomposition process.

"It excites the bacteria. They eat up the nitrogen, the pile heats up, and you get a double thrust." He shot his arm into the sky like a rocket. "I've had that pile go up to one hundred sixty de-grees. I've cooked eggs in that compost. You put an egg in a Ziploc bag and stick it four feet down in that pile and next morning, ten o'clock, you got a soft-boiled egg. If you want hard-boiled, you wait till noon."

Bricker boiled an egg that way on a TV garden show.

"We got so many complaints. All these people saying how obnoxious it was, that this was the grossest thing they'd ever seen in their lives."

Bricker shook his head in disgust. "I thought, *You dummies,* where do you think the egg comes from?"

Bricker found a cooked duck in there once. "My dog killed one of my best mallards and buried it in there."

I called up Ghann's a little bit later and asked the company president if he could explain why cricket manure was such compost gold.

"I don't know why," Clay A. Ghann said. "They eat a pretty good diet. We have our own secret recipe, if you will, similar to chicken feed, but with some special additives and vitamins. Maybe it's their internal workings."

Ghann said his father, Aubrey, started the company thirty-six years ago, in sort of the same spirit Bricker started his compost company.

"He was a welder and he was working on a dam out at Clark's Hill Lake, and when the dam was almost finished they were going to send him to the next job and he didn't want to move. He said, 'Well, this is a brand-new dam, there's gonna be a lot of fishing, so I'll give it a try.' "

It, of course, was growing crickets, which started to catch on pretty good after a few years. So good that Ghann's

Cricket Farm, at peak production, grows about 4 million crickets at a time. And that's about four tons of cc's a week.

"And it's good stuff. My father spreads it over his pasture—he's got a little farm about thirty miles from here, near McCormick, South Carolina—and boy, it turns that pasture a rich, dark green. You should see it on a lawn. It just makes stuff grow, plain and simple. Tomatoes, cucumbers, green peppers."

But cricket manure is just the fortuitous end product of the fish bait business, Ghann reminded me.

"When we have crickets left over, we dump 'em in the fish ponds up at the farm. We've got bluegills, catfish, bass. I tell people to stand behind the tree while they're baiting their hook, those fish are just that aggressive."

The Language of
the Heart

I was going back home for Father's Day and I didn't have a present, so I wandered around a mall looking at ties, and wallets and shirts. It all looked so anonymous, just the way I feel when I'm with my father. I've never hit it off with him. He likes my oldest brother best, my sister next, my second brother after that. Then me.

I can't stand feeling anonymous. So I went into a boutique and tried on a white jumpsuit I'd seen in the window. It looked better on the mannequin so I stuck my hip out and shot an arm up in the air. That was more like it, but I really couldn't walk around like that.

I put my old clothes back on, pondering the Father problem. Maybe a new recording of one of his favorite double concertos. (Thank you, he'd say. Let's compare it to my Shostakovich recording, the finest in the world.) Okay. How about some fine cheese? (Very good, he'd say. But remember that Stilton your brother used to bring down from Manhattan?) Have some more, Dad. Great for the arteries.

Could I knit a sweater vest overnight? My sister made a purple martin birdhouse one year. (I swear, he said, that girl can do anything she puts her mind to.)

I left the mall, without a present for Dad.

The problem is, our minds do not run along the same lines. We are not kindred spirits. We do not sit for hours at the kitchen table—as do my mother and I—smoking forbidden cigarettes and allowing our mistakes in life to take a philosophical turn.

So, I'd probably end up with the usual shirt that said nothing and everything about our relationship. The thought almost sent me into a roadside deli for a bag of extra-thick rippled potato chips, but I pulled into my favorite local nursery instead.

The wind was moving through the trees. No Muzak. A young man in old cutoffs and flip-flops was watering the vegetable seedlings and annuals with one of those rose attachments I wanted for my hose. We started talking about whether it was too hot to grow kale, and out of nowhere, an image from the past floated up: a vigorous vine overflowing with big purple flowers, planted by my father to camouflage a telephone pole at the edge of our yard.

"Do you have any clematis?" I asked.

We examined the ones he had: Comtesse de Bouchard, a rose pink with cream-colored stamens, Duchess of Edinburgh, with rosette-shaped double white blooms; *jackmanii*, a velvety purple . . .

But I knew what I wanted: sweet autumn (*Clematis paniculata*), a fragrant white flower that lasts through October. He had one tucked away in the greenhouse.

"Good choice," he said with an appreciative look.

I left with my Father's Day present, feeling beautiful, and headed for Maryland the next day. Driving down the New Jersey Turnpike, I watered my clematis out of Burger King cups and kept an eye on its little leaves through the rearview mirror. *Don't worry, Clem,* I whispered. *If he doesn't like you, I'll take you back.* We crossed the Delaware Memorial Bridge and hit the sweet humid air of the mid-Atlantic states.

I grew up on a farm surrounded by other farms, fields of corn and soybeans and herds of fat black Angus fenced in with hedges of wild rose. My great-grandfather was one of thirteen; he built the farmhouse when his own family outgrew the wooden cabin down by the spring. Family legend tells how Granddad saved the farm during the Depression by selling produce to wealthy Baltimoreans from his horse cart. They couldn't get enough of Grandmother's fresh cottage cheese. But Dad got restless with the country life: He went to college, made money in the city, came home to carve the meat and read the paper in the big chair that was saved for him.

It was Mother we talked to, pouring out our little childhood tragedies with the milk we drank ice cold from the fridge. When Dad appeared at the door, the weather changed. He laughed at our giant grape jokes—then corrected our grammar. He told us great stories—and expected us to do him one better. That air of competition always hung over the dinner table. Who could tell the funniest story. Who could really zing him one. Who won. It was never me. (That's *I*, Dad would say.)

Freshman year, I tried to explain Henry James to Dad. ("I never understood what he was talking about," he said.

"Where's the plot?") I wanted to wedge Mom's homemade pie down his throat, but I was the one who couldn't swallow. He was choking *me*, but I just sat there, feeling that old familiar torpor sweep over me. It comes from being in a place where you'll never be known. Like Dorothy in the poppy field.

But this Sunday was different. I set the clematis on the porch steps.

"Well, well," he said, stooping down to read the label. "Sweet autumn! That's the one with that lovely fragrance."

How strange to hear the word "lovely" on my father's lips. He straightened and took a deep breath. "Whoo," he said, softly, waiting for his heart to slow. He's seventy-seven, with a heart problem.

"Let's see, what's its Latin name? *Clematis* . . ."

"*Paniculata*," I said.

"That's it." He glanced at me through his bifocals.

We took a walk around the old grounds, proceeding slowly, in deference to his heart.

"What's that," I kept saying, but this time I really wanted to know.

"Spicebush. Or benzoin . . . we used to crush up the leaves and put it in the vaporizer when you couldn't breathe." (I know now why I couldn't breathe.) "It has those little yellow flowers in the early spring."

"Before the forsythia?" I asked.

"What about that, Mother?" he said.

"After," she said.

The old college prof paused. "By the way, for-SY-thia was named after William Forsyth, so it isn't pronounced for-SITH-ia, as everyone *insists* . . ."

I looked around for a heavy shovel. But he's so old now.

"Now fragrant viburnum's a good plant to put in up there," he said, switching the subject.

We took a breather by the rose beds, where some of the old varieties Grandmother planted still bloom.

"What's that one called?" I asked about a little low bush with pink blossoms.

"Oh heaven knows," he said companionably. "I *think* it's the original tea rose, from which the hybrid teas were grown, but I can't be sure. It's been moved so many times . . . and grown from slips, you know."

You know. The words of one kindred spirit to another. I just stood there, like a tender clematis, taking in the sun.

Mowing the Reel Way

When I moved into my bucolic shack on the river last fall, I didn't think about the little lawn problem. Or rather, the big lawn problem. A wide expanse of green that slopes down to the marsh. That's growing like mad in these summer rains.

In Brooklyn, I'd had a postage-stamp lawn that my reel mower took care of, perfectly well. It's a nifty Smith & Hawken five-blade cylinder, with cast-iron wheels and rubber tires, powered by sweat. Quiet and efficient, the catalog called it. No gas guzzling, no air pollution, no roaring motor to drown out the sounds of summer in the city, like the couple screaming at each other next door. Here was the politically correct machine.

A rotary mower and a reel mower are two completely different beasts. The rotary machine is the Godzilla of the lawn world. It works by whipping its blades through the grass and smashing the tops off. A reel mower, by contrast, is like an elegant seamstress. Its spiraled blades shear off the grass with the precision of perfectly sharpened scissors.

If properly adjusted, a reel mower—the sweat-powered variety—whirs across the lawn, deepening rather than laying waste to the peaceful afternoon: birds singing, dogs scratching, insects buzzing. The rotary mower roars over nature, belching fumes everywhere, until it stops, usually flooded, halfway across the lawn. Even if you get to the finish line, chances are, the lawn will have a brownish tinge the next day, because Godzilla has ripped off all the grass blades, leaving them ragged and torn, and open to infection. A reel mower, on the other hand, leaves the kind of clipped green lawn that inspired the croquet lovers of England to invent this machine in the first place.

Ahh. There are only a couple of problems.

"You're going to cut *this* with *that?*" Gary said, swallowing one of those snorts the natives around here reserve for ya-hoos from the city.

"Why not?" I said, trying to sound offhand. I'd already asked a high school kid to do it. But he and his power mower charge $35 a week. (But that's $140 a month, I said, in disbelief. I asked about once every two weeks. Oh no, he said. The grass would get too high and hard to cut. Oh, I guess I can't afford you. *Sorry*, I said. That's what living in the land of the rich and powerful does to you. You actually apologize for being poor.)

So anyway, there I was, Ms. Self-Sufficient of the Country Manse. Turning down Gary's offer to loan me his power mower. "You'd be done sooner. Then you could go rowing."

No, I paid 100 bucks for my little gem, and it was going to work, if it killed me. It did feel wonderful, at first, marching back and forth in the sunshine, still able to hear the scolding of the catbirds and red-winged blackbirds over the friendly clacking of my reel mower. And when my heart started working overtime, and the sweat poured down my face, and Gary and the tide and the rowboat came and went, I just told myself, Hey, that's what's wrong with people today. They all have motors or push buttons to do all the honest work for them, so they have to join a health club and eat nothing but broccoli to keep the pounds off. My reel mower does all that for free.

Gary came back, after an afternoon on the river.

"It's not getting the high grass," he said, leaning on his oar. We looked across the greensward, smelling so sweetly of fresh cut grass, lined with tall stands of weeds that my reel mower had just sort of squished and let pop right back up.

"I think the blades are dull," said Gary. "How do you sharpen this thing?"

In the gloaming of the afternoon, we read: "Your mower may be restored to its original cutting condition by a procedure known as lapping. This is done by switching the pinions and reversing the pawls so that the cylinder blades turn in reverse. . . ."

This is the kind of language that puts me to sleep if my life doesn't depend upon understanding it, and sends cold chills through me if it does. I think a well-cut lawn, in suburbia, lies somewhere in between. So I located some lapping compound at an auto supply store. I also snooped around town, asking about reel mowers.

First, nobody sharpens them anymore, because nobody has them anymore, because everybody has rotary mowers, which cut high grass.

So what did they use in the old days? I asked Charlie, of Eddie's Power Equipment. A scythe, he said.

This little project was turning into the Zen of Reel Mowing. Scything would be an enlightening activity. I could really get into my sweaty body rhythmically communing with the grasses. Meditation with my lawn, twenty minutes a day. Only at my speed, it would be all day, every day, which would make me a monk.

One evening Gary and I took apart the machine. It was liberating to learn how to reverse a pawl, and to get into ball-bearing grease. But my sharpened reel mower still just squished the big stuff.

"It's true, reel mowers don't cut tall grass, it's the nature of the beast," admitted Jack Allen, head of product development at Smith & Hawken, in California. "The reel has to reach the top of the grass and pull it back toward the mower bar, sweeping it across in a scissorlike action. But if the grass is very tall, it'll just fold it over."

Great, Jack. Maybe you should put that in the catalog. Jack made a note. Then he filled me in on the new catalog: the $250 silent reel mower, the $36 Austrian scythe blade, *The Scythe Book*, by David Tresemer, who waxes eloquently about the scythe. Did I know, for example, that Tolstoy devoted 118 pages to scything in *War and Peace*?

Funny you should mention it. I'd love to read that book, only I have to mow the lawn. And now I'll have to scythe the lawn. Unless I get a rotary mower. Then I can read about the old ways, in *War and Peace*.

What Cows Know

I buy my beauty cream at the Agway. They usually have what I'm looking for in the Tack Room, next to the horse liniment, or in dog and cat care, near the flea powder.

My brother-in-law introduced me to this fine product about six months ago, down in Maryland.

"Bag Balm?" I said, staring at the green can with the head of a cow surrounded by red clover blossoms. "They use this stuff on cows' udders."

"Eh-ah," said Rudy, a farmer's son from New Hampshire. "But it'll clear that poison ivy right up." He had to shout because a forklift was piling 100-pound bags of pig mash nearby.

My arm looked disgusting. People would glance at it and look away, as if I were a burn victim or a leper. It was an angry-looking, itchy mess that threatened to leave a scar.

I read the directions: "For chapped teats, superficial scratches, abrasions . . . Veterinary use only."

I opened the can. Yellow goop the consistency of axle grease, with the faint aroma of Band-Aids.

"Great, Rudy," I said. "Really attractive."

"Talk it to death, then," he said. Rudy only gives advice once. It's his Viking blood. Rudy of the North, we call him.

I bought the Bag Balm and gooped it on my arm. Now, I know this sounds like some born-again testimonial, but the itching and burning stopped. By the next day, it began to heal.

Winter came on, bringing with it the old reptile-legs syndrome. Cracks at the end of my fingers, little raw places around my cuticles. A face so dry it crinkled like paper when I laughed.

After a week of Bag Balming, those old reptile legs were kinda velvety. Brillo-pad hands soft as silk. Fewer wrinkles on my face. Band-Aids were beginning to smell sweet.

My women friends, the ones who usually buy placenta cream and stuff with shark oil or jojoba or almonds at Macy's, began to sneak into my bathroom. I'd hear the little tin lid come on and off. But I didn't mind. Bag Balm costs $4.95 for 10 ounces.

Lancôme's Noctosome Système Rénovateur de Nuit, which harmonizes with the skin's biological rhythms, costs $42.50 for 2.5 ounces.

"It's important to use it at night, when your body is at rest," said the saleswoman, who had to raise her voice over those ding-ding bells that are always going off in department stores. "When you're not working, or eating, or under any kind of stress, the cream can sink deep into the cells and make new ones," she said.

"How can a cream make new cells?" I asked, intrigued. Bag Balm couldn't do that.

"It stimulates them," she said, frowning at my face, which was dreadfully lacking, in the Lancôme department. I did a rough calculation.

Noctosome costs $17 an ounce. Bag Balm, 50 cents, and it even comes in cute little purse sizes. And besides, I needed some dog bones for Molly. I drove over to Agway.

"Oh yeah, people call us all the time, asking for Bag Balm," said store manager Joanne Pontrelli. They use it as a moisturizer, but the horsey set uses it on their horses.

There aren't many cows on Long Island, but the few there are know about Bag Balm. William Hsiang, who manages the 4-H farm in Riverhead, uses Bag Balm on his herd.

"Usually in the fall and winter, if we're milking, because it keeps their teats from getting chapped," he said. And yeah, he uses it on his hands, too, but he prefers Vaseline Intensive Care. Less greasy.

Bag Balm is manufactured by the Dairy Association Company of Lyndonville, Vermont, a little burg of 1,200, about thirty miles from the Canadian border, where winter temperatures can drop to 35 below.

"Mr. John N. Norris bought the recipe from a druggist about a hundred years ago," said Jean Hubbard, who manages the office up there. "It was called Kow Kare, and it had a vitamin-mineral supplement."

John N. Norris, Jr., seventy-three, runs the company now. Though he winters in Florida, where there's probably not much need for Bag Balm.

"Oh, that isn't true. It's good for sunburn, you know," said Mrs. Hubbard. Five people make Bag Balm, she said, in the little factory up the road, and its ingredients are simply petroleum jelly, lanolin and an antiseptic called 8-hydroxyline sulfate.

Most everybody up there, she said, uses it for chapped skin, cuts and bruises, sunburn and, well, a lot of other things that really shouldn't go in the paper. But if you insist.

"Everything from arthritis to bedsores, and hemorrhoids, diaper rash and nursing mothers, even quilters for the tips of their fingers," said Mrs. Hubbard, who personally answers about one hundred letters a week on the subject of Bag Balm.

The company doesn't advertise, and it stresses the "veterinary use only" line, but everybody knows it doesn't just make cows happy.

Dick Lawrence, forty-seven, used it for twenty-six years on the holsteins on his Vermont farm. Now he uses it for fixing faucets.

"You put a little Bag Balm on the pipe fittings, and tighten them up, and that's the end of the leak," he said.

Dermatologists even give it the nod.

"I use it myself," said Dr. Diane Maiwald of Huntington. "I came across it years ago, when I read it was good for severely chapped lips." Though, she said, you have to "prepare" the patients, who may not be used to filling a prescription at the farm supply store.

She said the active ingredient, also known as hydroxy quinoline sulfate, is basically used for the treatment of inflamed skin, dysentery and amoebic infections. And people can take high doses, with no ill effects. So smearing a little on your skin, at night, shouldn't hurt.

She adds, by the way, that the ritzy stuff, $40 and up, is the same basic idea as Bag Balm, or Crisco, for that matter. Only it goes on more easily than axle grease, and it smells better than Band-Aids.

Going Home Again

I wonder, as I sit in the maddest traffic jam of the year, heading south on the New Jersey Turnpike, if that first Thanksgiving wasn't a lot easier than the one I'm heading for. The first settlers died of exposure, scarlet fever, felling trees that fell the wrong way, eating the wrong wild nightshade plant. The survivors ate wild turkey and thanked the Lord for what they had. And what they'd left behind: unpaid taxes, failed businesses, starvation, jail sentences, all the relatives they didn't get along with.

We, on the other hand, are back in the mess our ancestors left in the Old World. There's no more wilderness to steal from the Native Americans. The empire we built on slavery is showing signs of collapse. The stolen land we farmed for generations is one big subdivision. We've polluted our air and water and chopped down our great forests. And most, if not all, of our relatives are within driving distance.

On Thanksgiving weekend, we travel hundreds of miles, brothers and sisters, aunts and uncles, nieces and nephews, converging on the old farm with pies and cheese and wine, fresh bread, new babies, cranky adolescents, new boyfriends, old friends closer than family, wondering nervously, as we wait for a congealed hamburger at the Molly Pitcher rest stop, what we will say to the brother or sister we haven't seen in years. Old bitternesses can surface so easily, carrying the gravy to the dining room, dropping some chance remark like a bomb on someone waiting to explode.

With that kind of attitude, no wonder you can't find a man. The way you want to be waited on, what woman would have you? Have you given up on having kids? Why can't you save money on that kind of salary?

Still we are drawn homeward, unable to erase our bloodlines. My father's nose sits on my own face; my sister's got my mother's smile. When I stand with my arm around my oldest brother, hip to hip, for a family snapshot, I revel in how tall and strong we are. Solid Pennsylvania Dutch stock, prone to gaining weight in our rear ends. We children, as old as we are, still feel the old twinges of envy: I wish I'd gotten her brains, I wish I'd gotten her body, why does everyone laugh at his jokes.

But the outrages of childhood seem far distant now, as I look into my father's eyes. I used to rail at his tyranny, shout that he didn't listen, but he listens more now, and so do I. We avoid certain subjects, on which no agreement can be reached. Because time is running out, and opening old wounds, at this point, only wastes time. Now I treasure each cup of coffee and conversation with my mother, because even as a child, I knew we had the same soul, and it hurts to see her so seldom.

My father was the first in the family to get a college education. And he traded working the fields for teaching physics in a little college town, ten miles from home. Where a black-haired young woman from the Eastern Shore learned how electricity works, and longed for a ride in his cream-colored roadster.

Eventually, the spark made a connection, and what a rakish couple they looked on their wedding day. What cute babies we were, in our high chairs and triangle party hats, when we were still incapable of unforgivable acts.

Then my grandfather's health began to fail, and Dad asked Mother if she would move back to the family farm, to help take care of the old folks, and the land his father and mother, and his father's parents before that, had tended without question. She said yes. When you love someone, life is no longer a question of the kind of house you want, the view you'd like, outside the kitchen window.

But the greater act of love was to come to live with another woman in the house, my father's mother, full of fun and smart as a whip, but strong-willed, used to having her own way. It wasn't easy for either woman.

And now my own parents are old. On Thanksgiving, as we mash the potatoes, and sneak more sugar into the cranberry sauce, and debate whether or not we could live without Brussels sprouts, we come to a harder question: How much longer Mom and Dad can stay in the old house alone. Whether or not one of us can take over the farm. And always, with stricken heart, I have to say, not now. Then Dad talks of selling, and moving into an old people's home, the fancy kind that takes all your money, for the privilege of a tiny apartment and a communal dining room, and doctors on call. Oh no we won't, says Mother. I'd rather keel over in the garden. Then she says, Do you think we should plant poplars along the north side, there, to hide those new houses?

After a heart-stopping feast, when we younger folks leave Dad to his nap, and Mom puts on her scarf, to walk with us, more slowly than she used to, down to the stream, we are all thinking of how not to let something important slip away. We hold hands, aunts and nephews, sister and brother, everyone keeping close to Mother, as we traverse the golden fields whose curves are as familiar as our own bodies, and ask, How could we keep the farm? Organic beef? A nature preserve? A writer's colony?

"You all have your own lives to live," my mother says. "You can't live for us." Yet her face, as she gazes into the brook, wants one of us to say yes.

My father once said, meaning to comfort me, "I came here with your mother because I loved the land, and didn't want to lose the farm. I used to think that was important. But I don't feel that way so much anymore."

I wanted to ask: So what is important, if not this, if not land and family? But I didn't. I don't know why.

After each family gathering, it is painful to go north again, struggling with emptiness and guilt, and the uncomfortable knowledge that I need, for family reasons, a different soil to grow in. Like seeds carried on the wind, some of us take root outside our native land. That is how the human race renews itself. Yet it feels so unnatural, and cruel; to abandon the ones you love, in order to love yourself.

Forbidden Poppies

I have discovered that I am a felon. You may be, too.

Anyone who grows that beautiful old poppy, *Papaver somniferum*, is breaking a federal law. Most of you probably know that, but don't care. Gardeners are independent sorts obeying natural laws.

Papaver somniferum is the opium poppy, the very one that filled the field that put Dorothy into such a deep sleep. The Sumerians called it the joy plant as early as 3000 B.C. Homer extolled its virtues in the *Odyssey*. For thousands of years, people have used it to relieve pain and turn anxiety into euphoria.

But to most of us, it's just a beautiful flower. (Though its potent abilities—and the fact that we are not supposed to have it—adds to its mystique.)

And so, we criminals keep passing the seeds over the garden fence.

"I think it's illegal to grow them," said my friend Rosemary, as she gave me a beautiful little box of seeds last Christmas. "But what are they going to do? Send the police into our gardens? They have no trust that anybody could be sensible."

(Really. We could easily poison somebody with a few rhubarb leaves or a little foxglove, but do we?)

She told me to scatter them over the snow in late February, because the seeds need the cold to break their dormancy. Choose a sunny, cultivated spot, she said, but don't do a thing in the spring. No weeding, no fertilizing. Poppies like to be left alone.

So one blustery day a year ago, I did what I was told, in my mittens. There's something great about a plant that embraces the dead of winter to give it life.

In the spring, the daffodils and tulips bloomed. I ate my first spinach salad. Still, the ground was bare. Duds, I decided. But poppies won't be rushed. Finally, in early May, a mass of tiny little pale green leaflets appeared. They were scalloped, like little loose-leaf lettuces, which is why some call it the lettuce-leafed poppy. (Or the hens-and-chicks poppy or the bread-seed poppy—other code names in subversive seed catalogs.)

Then the stems began to rise, their flower buds hanging down from crooked necks. Dozens grew to three feet high, and then, always at some moment I was never there (Rosemary thinks it's at night), the heads would rise and open—into beautiful saucer-shaped flowers with tissue-papery petals of lavender and deep wine. Some people have white and pink. Rosemary has heard of a garden of salmon-colored ones hidden somewhere on Long Island.

The flowers seem to float in the wind for days. Then the petals drift to the ground, exposing the pale green vaselike seed capsules.

In the late summer, the pods turn brown, and they are as eloquent as African sculptures, with tiny holes in their crowned tops, for the spilling of ripe seed. Nature thought of the saltshaker long before we ever did.

I shake the seeds out in the fall, and pass them on to renegade friends. It is an ancient ritual.

Since colonial times, people have mixed the gummy resin with a bit of whiskey to soothe a cough or an aching back. In *Gardening for Love* (Duke University Press, 1987), the late Mississippi gardener Elizabeth Lawrence tells how Confederate soldiers picked them in South Carolina gardens for laudanum.

Thomas Jefferson planted white opium poppies at Monticello. They grew in the historic garden near Charlottesville, Virginia, until last June, when they were yanked up.

"We had quite a go-round," said John Fitzpatrick, director of the Thomas Jefferson Center for Historic Plants. "After a drug bust at the University of Virginia, some local reporters started snooping around because they heard there were opium poppies at Monticello."

The center even sold the seeds. Until its governing board—"which has a mania for being legal," Mr. Fitzpatrick said—decided to press the issue.

Until then, nobody bothered to look over the garden fence. It was like those laws about sex. There just aren't enough officers to make sure everybody in the bedrooms is legal. And who cares, anyway?

A spokesman at the United States Department of Agriculture told me it was okay to grow them, though he couldn't cite the law. But go ahead, he said.

The board called the State Attorney General's office but couldn't get a firm answer. So they went to the Federal Drug Enforcement Administration.

"They pressed until they got a real answer, instead of 'Well . . . don't worry about it,' " Mr. Fitzpatrick said.

His tone was regretful. The whole thing irritates the director no end. "The fact is, you can drive down streets in this area and see them in people's gardens," he said. "Sure, it could be a dangerous plant. But so is every fourth plant in the garden."

(Yeah, like tobacco plants and all that rye used for whiskey. Why don't the feds go after them?)

Mr. Fitzpatrick compared his innocent poppies to guns: "Congress seems to buy the National Rifle Association's concept that it isn't guns that kill people. Well, the opium poppy doesn't hurt anybody, it's only what you do with it."

Hear, hear.

"Opium poppy seeds last a long time," Mr. Fitzpatrick said. "They could come in on the wind. And you would be a felon."

I scatter the seeds around the bare ground of the Maryland farm. Let them come and get me.

Garden Rhythms

I've noticed something about gardening. You set out to do one thing and pretty soon you're doing something else, which leads to some other thing, and so on. By the end of the day, you look at the shovel stuck in the half-dug rose bed and wonder what on earth you've been doing.

You've been gardening, an activity that doesn't necessarily lead directly to its supposed goal. This used to bother me, until I realized that this meandering—a kind of free association between earth, tools, body and mind—is the essence of gardening. What is supposed to be a practical, goal-oriented activity is actually an act of meditation.

For instance: All summer I've been thinking of planting some *Rosa rugosa*, the wild rose I'd grown to love on Nantucket. In June, the sandy dunes are blanketed in pink. And if you're on the steamer, you can smell the roses on the salt air—even before you enter the harbor.

This spring, when I moved to Long Island, that same heady perfume wafted over me on my first walk along the beach. It was a connection between disconnections, and I decided that when summer waned I'd go down to the beach and make some cuttings and try to grow *Rosa rugosa* along my garden wall. I figured a wild rose wouldn't demand regular nukings with pesticide—making it a good companion to my vegetables.

Another gardener had told me how simple it was to propagate: just wait until late summer, when the rose petals give way to rose hips, snip off some stems, dip them in rooting powder, plant directly in the ground and stick a restaurant-size mayonnaise jar over the top of each one, creating a kind of mini-greenhouse effect.

But doing something like this for the first time always makes me nervous. I suppose it's the terrifying gap between vision and reality. So I procrastinate, looking at too many books on propagation, asking too many gardeners for their advice. I make up excuses, such as "I've only found one mayo jar. I can't do this yet."

But then, along came this gorgeous fall day to yank me out of my inertia. It had rained the night before, but by morning the garden was splashing in golden light. The hollyhocks, the dahlias, the Brussels sprouts and tender Chinese cabbage all had a newly washed look. Everything had a sharp edge—even my coffee—as if a giant lens had brought the world into focus.

I picked up my heavy Craftsman shovel, enjoying its weight, the smooth wood of the handle. I hopped on top of the spade and sent the blade into the earth with a satisfying crunch. How nice it was to simply *dig*. Who needs Nautilus, with honest labor like this?

I was just working up a rhythm when something fluttered across the corner of my vision and disappeared in the trees. I felt sure it was a hawk. Something about its size, its swoop.

I rested a minute on my shovel and let my eye wander to the mass of weeds and long grass that had started out the summer as an herb garden. I'd made a mistake in planting— the herbs weren't in full sun, and their leggy, skimpy growth had depressed me, so I'd given up on them early on. But to-day, in this brilliant sunshine, I could bear to look beneath the weeds. I dropped my shovel and poked around in there. Figuring I had nothing to lose, I started yanking recklessly at the grass. I could smell oregano and lemon thyme, chives and something else I couldn't quite identify.

My neighbor Jane dropped by. We discussed getting to-gether that night for eggplant Parmesan—smothered in garden-fresh tomato sauce. I hopped over the garden wall to see how many of those dark purple beauties were left.

"Hey," a voice called out in a stage whisper. It was another neighbor friend of mine, standing near the manure pile, wav-ing his binoculars at me.

"There's a Cooper's hawk in the beech tree in back of your house," he said in a low voice.

I forgot about eggplants and followed him across the lawn.

"Up there," he whispered, handing me the binoculars. "On that branch to the left."

It takes practice to aim a pair of binoculars into a tree. You keep coming up with empty branches, blurry leaves. Finally, I found a big blob of brown and yellow. I turned the knob on the glasses, and the Cooper's hawk came suddenly into focus—its fierce red eyes staring straight into mine.

It had a flat head and a fishhook-sharp beak, a long gray

and white feathered tail. It was one of the most magnificent birds I'd ever seen. We just stood there, in silent admiration, until it flew away with a rather bored air.

I went back to my digging for a while, trundling cow manure back and forth in my sturdy blue wheelbarrow. The air was cool enough for a sweater, but the sun was just warm enough to make me wonder if I should take it off. I actually debated this great question. I admired the way the rubber wheels of my wheelbarrow jounced over the blue stones. These are the small pleasures that fill a gardener's mind. They seem trivial, but in a Zen world, they are the weave of life.

I started worrying about those mayo jars. I couldn't plant the roses without them—the tiny cuttings needed moisture to send out roots. My favorite deli had promised to save some for me—in return for a few flowers. So I cut a few bright yellow and red dahlias, some zinnias and cosmos, and took them downtown in a Mason jar.

I came out with a grin on my face—those flowers had really spiffed up the old bagel bin—and a couple more jars. Then I stopped by my local nursery for some rooting powder—and got into a conversation about *Allium giganteum*, whose gorgeous ball of lavender blooms in June. I came back to my car with a few bulbs—the size of tennis balls—and four Autumn Beauty sedums. Now *where* and *when* was I going to plant these?

On the way home, I stopped by the roadside to get a closer look at a flowering shrub I've just noticed—it sends cascades of star-shaped white flowers down the hillsides along my road and I don't know its name.

By now, it was four o'clock. I hadn't even gotten to the

beach to get those cuttings of *Rosa rugosa*. The so-called rose bed was just a long rectangle of overturned earth by the garden wall. And I had to work in the office all the next day.

Oh well. I'd get to it sometime. Now I had to cook up that harvest feast. I went into the garden to pick eggplants, peppers, basil and tomatoes. I stopped by the tangle of bean vines and sampled one of the Chinese asparagus beans. The shell was tough, so I opened it up to eat just the beans. They looked like the black-eyed peas I'd planted and forgotten about—because they'd never materialized. Now they were appearing as some kind of crazy hybrid. Another question growing in the garden: Had the two cross-pollinated?

By now I was a little exhausted. My dog, Molly, appeared, smelling dreadful, just like the dead thing she'd apparently just rolled in. So now she'd have to suffer the indignity of a bath—and I'd never get those roses planted.

But that's what I mean.

It had been a good day in the garden.

Sea Turtles

*T*he sea turtle, compared to Sir Isaac Newton, say, leads a rather insignificant life. Okay, so it's endangered, but what does it do all day, except swim in the ocean, feeding on crabs and mollusks and jellyfish, and basking in the sun on the water's surface?

So why would a thirty-two-year-old biologist named Steve Moreales spend every day, from July through September, out on a boat in Peconic Bay and thereabouts, tagging and tracking sea turtles? Moreales works for the Okeanos Ocean Research Foundation, which has a half-million-dollar grant to study sea turtles, especially the Kemp's ridley, which, for some mysterious reason, has started coming to Long Island from late June to early October, to feed, 2,500 miles from home.

Moreales says there are only about 400 nesting ridley females left in the whole world, which is quite a drop from forty-three years ago, when 40,000 dragged themselves up on a little stretch of sand on Mexico's Gulf Coast—thought to be their only nesting ground—on the very same day, to lay their eggs. A person witnessing such a thing could have walked for a mile across their backs, never touching the sand.

But now, the Kemp's ridley, and all sea turtles, who were swimming around before the dinosaur learned to walk, are in trouble. People steal their eggs, they kill them for meat and turtle soup, and turtle skins and jewelry. The Japanese stuff them, and hang them, as a symbol of longevity, an ironic little twist if you're a turtle. About 10,000 of them are killed a year, in the nets of shrimp fishermen, because the nets, which trawl for hours at a time, trap them beneath the water's surface. And turtles, just like people, have lungs.

So five years ago, when 58 Kemp's ridleys washed up on the North Shore, cold-stunned by the winter waters, it was an event, for turtle lovers at any rate. Most were dead, but 11 were revived and released, either down in Florida, or up here, when the waters warmed up, the following summer. And Okeanos set to work, following their movements and tagging any others they came across. Now, more than 100 fishermen call Okeanos if a turtle shows up in a net, and during the winter, a brigade of 248 volunteers walks the beaches looking for stranded sea turtles.

All for what? To learn about a mere reptile's life. What it eats, where it swims, how fast it grows. And when it leaves in the fall, how far south it swims. Imagine the tedium of such work, and its limitations. Moreales can track a sea turtle only as far as his transmitter can transmit. And when a turtle dives, just what he's doing down there on the murky bottom—probably eating—is conjecture. It would be like trying to do a field study of your neighbor, George, if you could only look in the kitchen window: Last night, George walked to the refrigerator at 11 p.m. He took out a quart of milk and poured it on a big bowl of Raisin Bran. Then he disappeared from the kitchen.

Your field book might ask: Did George eat the cereal in bed or in front of the TV? Does George do this every night, or only when he's depressed, or his wife is out of the house? Is this George's favorite food, or was he driven to eat the Raisin Bran because his main snack food (Snickers bars?) was depleted?

If you continued your research on George you might conclude that most of us swim around in the mysteries of life without having a clue to what's going on. We make a cup of coffee, put a sandwich in a Baggie and get on the Long Island Expressway. What great thoughts are we thinking, as the sign flashes "Delays ahead, Exits 41–44"? Maybe George is thinking, "Today, I'll try Northern State." Or, "Today, I'll divorce my wife." But he probably does none of these things. He just stays on the LIE, eats his sandwich, dumps the Baggie and comes home.

So George's life seems to be as uneventful as a sea turtle's. But if you study George, you may begin to understand him. Which is what Moreales is after with his turtles. And knowledge, and understanding, bring reverence for life.

Objectively speaking, the sea turtle's life is far more exciting than George's. If it survives. First of all, it's a miracle that a sea turtle even hatches, because so many eggs are eaten by wild dogs or people. And if it cracks through its shell—along with 100 or so brothers and sisters—there's no nice warm mommy to nestle against, because she's long gone, back to the ocean. Ancient instinct tells the hatchlings to swarm toward the light, which in dinosaur days was the moon and stars reflecting off the sea. But now, the sea is dimmed by high-rise condos and headlights and nightclubs, so instead of scuttling seaward, the baby turtles may head toward mankind—and death. If they do go in the right direction, many are eaten by hungry land crabs, and those who make it to their first wave are just so much food for fish. So it goes, for the sea turtle hatchling, whose odds of survival may be as low as 1 in 10,000. He has to watch out for oil spills and nets, and trappers, and even George's plastic bag, which he might mistake for a jellyfish, his favorite food. Only plastic bags don't slide down as easily as jellyfish. They plug up his system, and he dies, slowly, of starvation.

Meanwhile, what is old George up to? The usual. Driving to work, thinking about taking the Northern State, or getting a divorce, or eating his sandwich. And when, like the turtle, George's life takes a sudden turn, and he's lying by the side of the road, suffering a heart attack (too much fatty food? anxiety about sea turtles?), who cares? Well, the people who know George, the ones who have been tracking the little tragedies and comic moments of his life.

To the rest of us driving by, George's death means as little as the life of a hatchling, crushed by a passing car, because it scuttled toward the wrong light. In the eyes of the universe, both hold the same weight. Whether you love a man or a sea turtle depends upon how much you know about his journey.

Coexisting

I have whiteflies in my greenhouse. I can keep the population down with Safer's soap, but they're still there, laying their tiny eggs on the undersides of leaves and flying up in little white clouds if I shake their favorite plants.

Whiteflies are something gardeners have to live with. The standing joke is, they come with the seeds. But now that I've started my empire of flower and vegetable seedlings, I'm getting nervous. Imagine: a whole garden of tomatoes, peppers, eggplants, hollyhocks, nicotiana, cleome, literally sucked to death. Gorgeous flowers flopping over like wan brides of the vampire. Bright green tomato vines turning yellow before they die.

Whiteflies thrive on the lifeblood of plants. The eggs, laid on the undersides of leaves, hatch into yellow crawlers who stick their little beaks into plant tissues and suck the food right out of them.

So letting whiteflies get out of control is like renting the guest room to Count Dracula. And as an organic gardener, I get scared sometimes.

"Safer's won't do the trick," said a young man at my neighborhood nursery. "I'd go for something like Cygon or Orthene, systemics that really do the job."

He handed me a bottle of Cygon 2E, which has a big WARNING on the front. "Why fool around? You want to get rid of the problem."

I looked at the bottle. I read the label on the back: "Birds and other wildlife feeding on treated areas may be killed. Keep out of any body of water. Highly toxic to bees exposed to direct treatment or residues on crops." It also said, "Ornamentals only."

"Wait a second," I said. "This is just for ornamentals. I'm growing vegetable seedlings."

"Oh yeah, you wouldn't use this on vegetables," he said. "You'd die." Which may be an exaggeration, but Cygon does kill guinea pigs and rats in laboratory studies. And I'm not so far from a rat that I'll volunteer for a guinea pig.

I'm not villainizing the young man at the garden center. He's a graduate of a respectable agricultural school, he was trying to be helpful and he shares that very American love of the "good, clean" approach: Nuke 'em good and get it over with.

It was suddenly quite clear to me how easy it is for the average gardener, a little nervous about losing a crop, to run into the garden center and pick up the first thing the salesclerk recommends. But maybe we'd better stop acting like sheep.

I use Safer's for a number of reasons. It's safe. It won't give me cancer. It won't get into the groundwater. It won't kill a bumblebee or a bird or a fish. It's in harmony with why I garden in the first place—to celebrate life.

I've also decided to do what I can to stop poisoning my own backyard. Our groundwater is polluted, thanks to chemical fertilizers, insecticides and herbicides. There aren't very many earthworms, or bumblebees, or ladybugs around anymore. Ever wonder why? Because of our American love affair with the quick fix. With the clean green lawn with nary a weed or a grub. With the perfect, unblemished tomato.

Things are getting better. A landscape contractor in Hempstead halted pesticide spraying more than two years ago. County extension offices are giving courses in integrated pest management—a philosophy that advises monitoring insect populations and using a combination of the least toxic controls that will still result in a healthy plant.

Which brings me back to whiteflies. If I can tolerate spritzing them with soap every week or so, a time-consuming activity—and if I can tolerate the thought of not *eliminating* them from the face of my little patch of earth—Safer's is just fine. But feeling it's fine or not fine is an attitude thing that runs very, very deep. As deep as our aquifers, from which I've decided not to drink.

Have you ever tried to find out what a pesticide like Cygon or Orthene or Malathion actually is? How quickly it breaks down? Whether it accumulates in the food chain? Whether it gets into the groundwater? I called my local county extension office and spent all afternoon, with various agents, trying to decipher hieroglyphics like "O, O-Dimethyl S-(N-methylcarbamoylmethyl) phosphorodithioate (56)," which is Cygon. It's an organophosphate, which breaks down faster than an organochlorine. Its "dermal LD 50" for guinea pigs is larger than 1,000 milligrams per kilogram. Its "oral LD 50" for rats is from 500 to 600 milligrams. Which means a two-pound guinea pig would need 1,000 milligrams of Cygon smeared on its skin, and a rat would have to eat 500 milligrams, before they croaked. Which sounds like it's better to use Cygon for hand lotion than as a mixer. LD 50, by the way, means lethal dose for 50 percent of the animals tested. Is everything perfectly clear now? You can see why people don't ask a lot of questions.

That's my job. I've read that the whitefly parasite, *Encarsia formosa*, is an excellent biological control for whiteflies. So I called the Natural Gardening Research Center in Sunman, Indiana, and learned that getting them established is tricky. If the average temperature in my greenhouse gets much below 70 degrees, *Encarsia* won't breed fast enough to keep up with the whiteflies. *Encarsia* breed like bunnies over 75 degrees— but that's a little hot for sturdy vegetable seedlings.

I also learned that I'd need three sets of 100 *Encarsia*, at $6.50 each, to be sent at two-week intervals, to establish a healthy population of larvae and adults. But would they stick around after feasting on the whiteflies?

"As long as they have something to feed on," the woman on the phone said. "If not, they'll die out. That's why you'll need some BugPro, which is our artificial diet for beneficial insects." That was $19.50 for the bugs, and $7.50 for two pounds of bug food. A big bottle of Cygon is under $12.

Next I called BIRC, Bio-Integral Resource Center, in California, to find out how and if *Encarsia* really work. BIRC's executive director, Sheila Daar, had some interesting information: "The adult *Encarsia* is a winged mini-wasp that flies to the underside of a leaf and, using its antennae, beats on the leaf like a drum until it finds the third-stage larva, or the pupa," she said. "Then it inserts an egg into the pupa, which hatches into a worm stage inside the whitefly. It eats the whitefly and turns the pupae black, so gardeners can tell with the naked eye if the whiteflies are getting parasitized."

Encarsia don't seem to ever eat all the whiteflies, she said, so I didn't have to worry about them starving to death.

So I've ordered some *Encarsia*, and I'll let you know how they work out. Meanwhile, it's on with the Safer's. Insecticidal soaps work by breaking down the protective oils on an insect's skin, which makes it dehydrate. Ivory soap will do the same thing, but the problem is, it can kill good bugs as well as bad. Safer's soap is made of fatty acids which have been selected for specific insects. So you can dump some on a ladybug and she'll live.

Naming Things

We share the biosphere with about 5 million different kinds of organisms, so it's a good thing we've given them names. Imagine trying to keep track of stuff without naming it. We'd be in a great big, 5-million-thing state of confusion.

What if people just said, "I smelled this beautiful thing in the thing and it reminded me of a thing. It wasn't at all like the thing my thing used to call a thing. So which thing is it?"

I was thinking something like this the other day, as Bill Barash led me about the Planting Fields Arboretum in Oyster Bay, pointing out how some things that don't look at all like other things are actually in the same family of things. Barash, an assistant horticulturist, acts as the arboretum's taxonomist—labeling all the trees and bushes around the place—so he has to be pretty clear about naming things. Just now, he was speaking Latin.

Naming Things

"*Digitalis* and *Antirrhinum* are in the Scrophulariaceae family," he said, staring at a tall, gorgeous foxglove with freckles. Just speak English, I thought. Why not just say that foxglove and snapdragons are in the figwort family?

Barash was peering into a flower now. After sixteen years here, he's gotten kind of intimate with the residents.

"If a flower has an ovary above the sepals or petals, it's called superior," he said, plucking a blossom from its stem. "If the ovary is below the petals, it's inferior."

We examined it closely. Definitely superior. We peeked inside the lavender-freckled corolla and counted four stamens, those little columns that are covered with pollen. Two of the stamens were longer than the other two—a seemingly small fact of great enormity to botanists.

"Snapdragons also have a superior ovary, and two sets of stamens, with two different lengths," said Barash. "That's a clue to the Scrophularia-ce-ae family."

He had to screw up his mouth to say that, but he did so with satisfaction. "Veronica is in the same family," he said. So next time you pull this weed out of your lawn, check out its stamens.

I suppose this isn't a very sexy subject to most people, but actually, these plant families are based on sex. Or at least the great Swedish naturalist Carolus Linnaeus thought their sexual differences—their stamens and pistils—important enough to use as the basis of his binomial classification system, which he published in *Species Plantarum*, in 1753.

He wasn't the first guy to organize things. A Frenchman named Joseph Pitton de Tournefort had already come up with the idea of the genus or family fifty years before. In *How Plants Get Their Names*, L. H. Bailey tells how Tournefort divided the plant world into two groups—trees and herbs.

Then he divided these into groups that had flowers and groups that didn't. Then he made divisions by flower shapes.

Tournefort was like the first person who looked around the church and said, "Hey, everybody in the Jones' pew has ears that stick out."

But Linnaeus went even further. You should have seen his kitchen drawers. He gave everything two names. The first name was the genus name, the second, the species. And he used stamens and pistils to create the families. The system was dubbed the "sexual system," and it brought together many related plants—and also, as Bailey points out, it "divorced many natural relationships."

But flawed or not, it was the first time that everybody knew what everybody else was talking about, if, that is, they talked in Latin. Nobody had to wonder anymore if a fairybells was the same thing as deadmen's bells. They could just say, "Oh yeah, that's *Digitalis purpurea*." If they sounded a little stuffy, at least things were clear.

And it's interesting that *Digitalis* comes from the word "digitus," which means finger. The Romans, then, weren't so very far from the English peasants, who looked at this flower and called it fairy thimbles and folks glove, or from kids today, who are still sticking foxglove blossoms on their fingers and pretending to be witches. I used to do the same thing with long, pointy, orange trumpet vine blossoms.

"Is trumpet vine in the scrofu-scrofamagig family?" I asked Barash, who was now dragging me over to a crab apple and telling me that this tree was actually a rose. "No, trumpet vine is in another family," he said. "You can't always go by the shapes of the flowers."

I see. It just depends on who's organizing the drawers.

We stood beneath the crab apple, which was laden with white blossoms tinged in pink. We counted five delicate, satiny petals. We noted the "inferior" ovary, below the petals, which will turn into the rose hip or fruit come summer's end. It did look like *Rosa rugosa*, in a way. Except that it was a tree.

It was a lovely walk, past flowering quince and weeping cherry, amelanchier and pear. All members of the Rosaceae family.

"The entire family is edible, so you can eat the flowers of the apple, pear, strawberry," said Barash. "Some people call the strawberry the edible rose."

We walked on, past some luminous blue delphinium, which is in the Ranunculaceae, or buttercup, family.

" 'Rana' is Greek for frog, and many buttercups grow in swampy areas," said Barash.

I never thought that a blue delphinium looked much like a yellow buttercup, but both have five petals and lobed leaves, a dead giveaway for the frog family. And next time you admire a clematis vine or a columbine, take a look at the leaves. Lobed, which means Ranunculaceae. To some people.

Barash pointed out a little spindly tree that didn't look like much to me, but it sent the plant man into a rhapsody.

"*Oxydendrum arboreum*," he said. " 'Arboreum' means woody, and this tree does everything. Its wood is used to make hammers in pianos, spools for thread. It's slow-growing, and small, which makes it good for suburban yards, and it has a beautiful lily-of-the-valley-shaped flower in mid-summer, and its leaves turn burgundy in the fall."

Oxydendrum is a member of the Ericaceae family. So is *Enkianthus*. We brushed by a huge specimen whose pearly white drops were shaped much like those of a low-growing pink heath farther down the path. The little bells reminded me of blueberry blossoms, and all are in the same family. Ericaceae.

"Of course, azaleas and rhodies are in the same family, which sort of throws a wrench into the works," he said blithely. "But they all have the same leathery evergreen leaves."

I stuck my nose into a drooping Japanese andromeda, *Pieris japonica*, and inhaled its pleasant, spicy fragrance. I suddenly felt hungry.

"Tacos," said Barash. "It smells like tacos."

So where's the taco in the binomial system of classification? Did Linnaeus have a cold or what? Had he never tasted a taco? It was suddenly clear how arbitrary organization is: If a gourmand had been running the show, instead of a sex maniac, maybe we'd have a plant called *Pieris taco*.

Little Miracles

I got a call the other day that got me to thinking about miracles.

It was one of those electric-blue-sky days when nobody should be in the office. I was staring out my window at the flaming red *Euonymus* bushes that flank the parking lot at *Newsday*, and at my brand-new flaming red truck, which was sort of waving at me and suggesting that we should sneak off to the beach. Meanwhile, the woman on the phone was talking rather excitedly about Easter lilies.

"I'd just been to a wake for my friend's mother, Frances, who was eighty-three, and I'd given a donation to the Franciscans in her name, and the next day I went to the crafts fair at St. Francis Church in Levittown. We were walking toward the statue of St. Francis, and I see these lilies," said Rita Sands O'Keefe. "My friend said, 'Am I seeing things or what?' "

Whoever heard of an Easter lily blooming near Halloween? O'Keefe took it as a sign.

"It was sort of mystical. I was hoping that maybe I'd win the lottery or something good would happen," she said. O'Keefe said she is a spiritual person. She's experienced things that, once related to some people, make them think she's a nut. Like the time she heard her first husband, James, whistle, the day after he'd died.

"I was upstairs resting and I heard Jim's whistle come up the stairs," she said. I was still looking at the electric-blue sky, but I was thinking that people often experience these things when their loved ones die. It's a way of keeping reality from crashing in too fast and killing you.

O'Keefe said the whistle came right out of a triptych of the Crucifixion, the Ascension and the Resurrection sitting on the bedroom dresser.

"I said to my mother that somehow Jim was with me, that he was never going to leave me. And I still have the feeling he's there, even though I'm remarried now."

Then O'Keefe hinted that her life wasn't very happy right now, and that the Easter lilies were trying to tell her that life was about to take a turn for the better. Then she had to hang up because the man who'd come to put down new kitchen tiles was at the door.

I went to the library to find a Bible.

Matthew 6: . . . And which of you by being anxious can add one cubit to his span of life? . . . Consider the lilies of the field, how they grow; they neither toil nor spin; yet I tell you, even Solomon in all his glory was not arrayed like one of these. But if God so clothes the grass of the field, which today is alive and tomorrow is thrown into the oven, will He not much more clothe you, O men of little faith?

Jesus was telling people not to bother themselves with material worries. Don't give a second thought to Wall Street, because God will take care of it, if you keep the faith. But you can also read that passage differently. If God is going to throw the grasses of the field into the oven, will He or She or It not throw you in the oven, too?

I drove over to the Episcopal St. Francis of Assisi Church in Levittown. And there, blooming right near the statue, were the Easter lilies. St. Francis had his hands, palms together, raised in prayer toward the sky. The lilies were waving in the chilly fall air.

Rev. Robert H. Walters said the potted lilies had been planted outside after flanking the altar on Easter Sunday.

"I can't remember whether those were put in this year or the year before, but they've been blooming for a week or so," he said.

I wanted to think this was a miracle, but, out of duty, I called the New York Botanical Garden.

"It's not so uncommon," said propagation manager Len Marino. "In fact, it's relatively easy to get Easter lilies to rebloom. Once the flowers have faded and fallen, you treat the plant as a potted foliage plant. Give it water and fertilizer. Cut the stem back, but leave a portion with foliage on it. That'll provide food for the bulb and help it mature. It'll continue to grow and strengthen, especially in a garden situation, where it has room to establish itself. By August or September, the plant may well send up a new flower spike."

Darn. I'd wanted something inexplicable. Not just *Lilium longiflorum* doing its thing.

I thought about what Rev. Walters had said: "Some people are attuned to a certain kind of spirituality. And when there is a confluence of events—such as the death of this friend named Frances, and then the lilies blooming next to St.

72

Francis—these people are likely to see those events as more than just a coincidence. Others would see it as pure chance."

What's the value of going through life seeing signs in common events? I decided to ponder this question at the beach. I waded in the ocean. The water was miraculously warm. I looked at what the fishermen were catching. I breathed the salt air. I wasn't at work. Some people would call this playing hookey. I called it a miracle.

Take St. Francis, for instance. The son of a wealthy cloth merchant of Assisi turned in his war gear for beggar's clothing after he heard a voice coming from a crucifix in the rundown church of San Damiano. The voice said, "Go and repair my house, which you see is falling down." Somebody else would have just figured he'd had too much vino the night before—and put his armor back on. But St. Francis called it a vision, and look what he accomplished.

Or how about that *Euonymus* outside my office window? Some people call it a burning bush. Maybe it told me to go to the beach.

Rita Sands O'Keefe, I am not making fun of you. I am thinking about how we all look for signs in the universe. And why should we not?

Some people believe that God makes the lilies bloom. This gives them strength to face the tile man in the morning. Some people say it's just botany. That's enough of a miracle for them.

But I think we're all hoping, secretly or not, for something inexplicable. So that we can stop worrying all the time, stop taking total responsibility for everything. So that we can say, once in a while, and really mean it, that the burning bush made me do it.

My Old Dog

$\mathcal{T}$he spinach and the lettuce are up, but instead of feeling all happy and excited, I'm getting nervous. I look at the half-pound bag of Tendercrop beans with a sense of dreary fatalism. Maybe there's no sense in even planting them.

"You should have seen him waddling out there every evening, as if that lettuce patch were his personal garden," my mother said. "You'd think we planted those string beans last year just for him. He ate every one."

My mother loves string beans. But our Maryland ground-hog loves them more.

"Sometimes I'd be out there when he came out of his hole over by the lilacs, and he'd just sit there, waiting for me to leave," she said, holding her hands up to her chest in an admirable imitation of a groundhog.

There was a silence as we gazed at Molly, our watchdog,

our ferocious fur ball who wags her tail at all creatures great and small. Oh sure, in her youth she used to charge after squirrels and rabbits. But she'd skid to a stop at the very moment her lips touched fur. She wasn't trying to eat them; she was trying to herd them.

Molly is a twelve-year-old Saint Bernard squished into a setter's body with some collie blood thrown in. But since this isn't exactly Big Sky country, she has to make do with humans. A few hours after sundown, when everybody's still kicking around downstairs reading and trying to stay out of the ice cream, she sits at the bottom of the stairs and whines, trying to get us into our stalls for the night. When that doesn't work, she heaves an enormous sigh and goes up to bed herself.

My cat, Mrs. Grey, isn't any better. I planted a jillion crocuses last fall and hardly a one came up. But there were a lot of mouse holes.

"Look at those holes!" I shouted at Mrs. Grey and Molly last weekend. They gave me blank stares as they sat, rumps together, on the old cement terrace. They like to sun themselves out there like two old folks at a retirement home.

"I'm going to get a new dog," I keep telling Molly. "One of those little terriers bred to go down rat holes."

But she knows I can't stand little dogs.

"A Labrador, then," I say. "They make excellent hunters."

But my heart isn't in it. I am a one-dog person and a one-cat person; I don't make attachments easily.

In fact, when I moved from Long Island to New York City last summer and brought my animal friends down to the farm, they adjusted much better than I did. At first they suffered, getting jittery when I repacked my bags on Sundays, trying to sneak in the back of my truck if I left the door open.

"They miss you terribly," my mother said the first weeks I was away. "They sit on the cement staring at the driveway, as if you'll be turning the corner any minute."

Which made me feel kind of empty and sad, like a woman who'd abandoned her children for her career. But I knew they wouldn't have liked the city. The last time Molly lived in an apartment, she sat by the front door all day, as if her dog door would materialize.

But when I saw how they took to the farm, I almost felt worse.

Mrs. Grey spent the cold days of February on the Victorian velvet couch in the living room, curled up on a handmade afghan. And Molly, initially banned to the kitchen at night, was soon snoring on the floor by my mother's bed.

And she's gained a few pounds.

"I couldn't get the hang of just sticking that pill down her throat," my mother said. "So I wrap it in liverwurst or a hot dog." Molly gives me a look from beneath the kitchen table. It's *their* way now.

And now I couldn't crowbar these two away from my mother. Mrs. Grey kept my mother company during the Olympic Games this winter. "She'd sit up when the figure skaters came on," Mom said.

Oh, they're glad enough to see me when my friends and I show up on weekends. They wander out to the garden to watch us dig, and to dig holes themselves. When I say "Sit!" it's usually on a new transplant.

We still take long walks together and Molly will sleep at

the foot of my bed when I'm there. But when it's time for me to go, she doesn't sit by the car door anymore.

The days are gone when we used to go for five-mile runs down Long Island's sandy roads. Molly's got a touch of arthritis in her shoulder and the last time we tried to run, she limped home. Now her back legs are giving out.

Just last week, I invited her to come for a ride with me, and she trotted to the driver's side to hop up and over to her usual place on the passenger's side. But this time, her back legs collapsed and she crumpled to the ground with a hurt, embarrassed look on her face.

I tried to lift her in, but she balked, and slunk back into the house, seeking solace under the kitchen table. I drove into town alone, missing her doggy presence as sharply as I still do in the city. I've had her since she was a puppy. She shared my marriage and my divorce, a couple of hard moves and a lot of little lonelinesses. And now she is growing old without me. And the groundhog is running amok.

The only answer is a .22, my brothers say. Havahart traps are just hypocrisy: catch an animal in a trap and let it out near somebody else's garden—or take it to the Humane Society to be killed.

But our groundhog is not going to evaporate. Unless we put up a fence that makes the place look like Alcatraz, he will get into the lettuce and the beans.

I look at Molly, asleep under the table. Her paws are twitching, and she's emitting these little woof-woofs, which means it's a pretty exciting dream chase. Maybe she's catching a Mint Milano.

Growing Old

$\mathcal{M}$y mother and I watched an old movie on TV as my father lay in a hospital bed ten miles from home, hooked up to a bunch of tubes that are supposed to be saving his life.

"She's so radiant," said my mother, as Greta Garbo danced with Fredric March at the ball, and we knew it was only a matter of time before Anna Karenina would leave her husband, the sickeningly cold Basil Rathbone.

"Yeah," I said companionably, as we finished off the cognac and smoked another cigarette. We were indulging ourselves, escaping from the day, and the stark image of my father, alone in his sterile room. And the operation he would soon have.

I wanted to ask my mother if she'd ever had an affair. But I didn't, of course, and the moment passed.

I went down to the old family farm last week, to help my parents out. My father had fallen in the middle of the night, and my mother hadn't been able to lift him off the floor. She'd called 911 and the ambulance came right away, she said. You don't have to come down, she kept saying, because they're just monitoring his heart.

"Fine-tuning" it, they say, which is a euphemism for re-adjusting the megaton of drugs that keep my father alive—and poison him at the same time. Modern medicine is so jolly. There's no such thing as just lying down in your rose bed, and dying, when things wear out.

I'm fine, she kept saying on the phone. I'll let you know when I need you.

But I imagined her there, alone, driving her old car back and forth from the hospital, worrying every minute about the knock in the engine, counting the days until she could pick up the new Chevy. Trying not to worry about the bills, and the pile of papers on my father's desk. At seventy-seven, it's hard to take over the finances, when your husband has handled all that.

I didn't take her word for it, that she was fine. I went down anyway, like a mother coming after a child. And to my surprise, she let me pamper her. Cook all the food she loves, that my father won't eat. Pour her a bit more scotch, because with Father gone, there was no hurry to get dinner on the table. She said this with an air of surprise. Like someone taking her first breath of air on a tropical island. She missed him. But she didn't miss the tyranny of his needs.

They've stayed on in the big old farmhouse, on land where the corn still grows tall. The Lippy boys farm it for them, though they aren't boys anymore. And a caretaker keeps the grounds up. His wife helps my mother in the house. But a couple weeks ago—before my father fell—they quit. At eighty-one, he isn't an easy man to work for.

My parents didn't tell us that this tenuous lifeline—that allows them to stay on the farm—had been broken. And they didn't ask us for help.

"Don't worry about it," my father said, when my sister came home a few weeks ago, to find the grass too tall, the roses dying, the house collecting dust.

"We'll sell the farm. Go to a retirement home," he said, which is what he always says when the caretaker threatens to leave. Only this time my mother said, "I won't go."

It used to be such a beacon of light, that house. So many rooms for friends, the living room alive with music, the dinner table laden with roast beef and potato rolls, vegetables from the garden, the wine and coffee and chocolate we brought from the city. Fireflies lighting up the dusk that lay so dreamily under the maple trees.

Now, the house of our childhood is an aging soul, with wheezing pipes and trees so old they could fall on the roof. It hovers over its ancestral ground like a question: Why do children have to leave?

Because they have to, to live. But sometimes, it seems to me, wood and mortar and soil take their own revenge. Matching ruthlessness with ruthlessness. Grass grows ominously fast when you're too old to cut it down. Roofs cave in when you can't climb up to fix them.

My father's rose beds were a shambles. The leaves covered with black spot, or skeletonized by the Japanese beetles, who had chewed up every blossom and bud.

I drowned them in a coffee can half-filled with kerosene. And then went to the woodshed, to my father's collection of poisons. That day, an organic gardener declared chemical warfare in an old man's honor. And in a few days, I had some roses to bring to my father.

See, Dad, I said. Your roses are coming back. How about that, he said. Then he started to argue, this shadow of himself, about the new car.

He'll come through this one all right. But I'm not so sure about my mother. When he comes home, there she'll be, fixing his every meal. Keeping a constant ear cocked when he's out of sight. Has he fallen? Has he stopped breathing? Can she go to the store, or out to a rare lunch with friends, without him collapsing? Like he did the other night.

The caretaker and his wife are back, thanks to delicate negotiations. And the new car has arrived. So everything is fine, as we say in our family, for now.

But I wonder what will happen to the neat file of numbers I left with my mother. For the hospital social worker. And the council on aging. And the private "home care" companies, which charge $40 an hour for a registered nurse and $15 an hour for a nurse's aide. We're the kind of family that doesn't cotton to outsiders. Besides, if you're used to asking one person for everything, and getting it, why change?

In the evenings, I call home and ask how it's going. Your father's doing well, Mother says. And the new car is wonderful.

That's good, I say. Knowing that it isn't good. To let her handle everything. To let her drive the car, new or not, at night, when she's tired, and her vision is bad.

But we have our own lives, my mother has always said. And we'll ask for your help when we need it.

And so we children just go on living our own lives, until another beam falls, from a house we thought would stand forever.

Late Again

I woke up at three the other morning with a headache. I practiced deep breathing to stave off an anxiety attack. But I couldn't get that voice out of my head: *Your leeks are late. Your leeks are late. You haven't ordered your potatoes yet.*

Have you ever had a steaming bowl of leek and potato soup on a cold December evening, made from home-grown potatoes and leeks dug that very day from the frozen ground? Leeks are milder than onions, and they sweeten in the icy earth. And a potato has an earthy, primeval flavor that's hard to describe to the supermarket palate.

Eating a garden-grown potato is like stuffing a piece of earth in your mouth. It's as if you can taste the minerals and nutrients the plump little tuber has taken from the soil. Eating a potato is as close as you can get to the land.

I lay there, having a soup vision. Leeks and potatoes, combined in a homemade chicken stock, blended to a creamy mixture, but not too creamy. It's important to have just enough lumps to recall the potato, so that a big spoonful makes you feel humble, peasantlike, close to the gods.

The muscles in the back of my neck were turning to high-tension wire. I'd missed the boat again. You're supposed to start leek seeds indoors about two months before planting out. Some planting charts say *three* months. I felt angry, resentful and sleepless. Gardening is supposed to be relaxing. But there I lay, in the deep midwinter, feeling *behind.*

Stay calm, stay calm, I told myself. Let's see: Mid-February to mid-March, that's one month. Mid-March to mid-April, that's two months. So, depending upon which chart you go by, you could plant them out between the middle of April and the middle of May. Middle of May? That's almost tomato planting time. Isn't that too hot for leeks?

I sat up in bed. I pulled out *Making Vegetables Grow* by Thalassa Cruso, whose practical voice always calms me down. "The leek is, incidentally, the national emblem of Wales," she told me. I wondered when they started leeks in Wales. Probably months ago. I read on. There it was, in bold letters: "Three months before the last spring frost."

My headache crawled up the back of my neck and settled behind my eyeballs. I hate mention of the last spring frost. You drive yourself crazy trying to decide just when that is. Some say mid-April, some say mid-May. But it really depends upon how near the water you are, and whether you're on the South or the North Shore, and whether your garden is up on a hill or down in a valley, and whether it snuggles up next to some nice warm south-facing wall or sits naked and alone in some field, exposed to all the pernicious elements of early spring.

But I'm hedging here. In my heart, I know that my own

garden's last frost date is mid-April. I know that I should have planted those leek seeds in January. Just like the late James Crockett advises. And Thalassa Cruso as well.

Well, farewell, former favorite garden writers. My new hero is Bob Thomson, Crockett's successor to the Victory Garden. The Massachusetts nurseryman has just come out with *The New Victory Garden*, and in it I found my salvation: "I start my leek crop indoors in late February," Thomson writes. "In four-inch pots filled with soilless medium I sow the seeds and cover them with ¼ inch of the medium, then bottom-water until the pots are moist all the way from top to bottom. The pots are set onto my heat pad at 75 degrees, which will produce seedlings in seven days."

Thank you, Bob. I gazed at the color photograph of the dark green shoots, all coming up straight and tall in their four-inch pots. My head stopped throbbing. Giant Mussel-burgh and Titan are Bob's favorites. Now they're mine, too. We late-leek lovers have to stick together. I'd put in my order tomorrow. I'd run down to Flowertime for the four-inch pots.

I read on, overjoyed at the following: "I used to rush the leeks into the spring garden as soon as possible, but I no longer do that. One year, in a scheduling mix-up"—I loved him for admitting he'd flubbed—"I let the leeks remain indoors until early May, about three weeks after the last frost date in this area. When I finally got them into the garden, I didn't have much hope for a good crop. Surprise: They turned out to be the best leeks I'd produced in the Victory Garden. Now my practice is to keep those seedlings growing indoors well into May, to give them the longest head start possible. My new rule is that bigger transplants grow the best leeks. The February start indoors, coupled with three months

of indoor growing time, gives me those big, healthy transplants."

I pictured Giant Musselburgh's creamy stalks, over eighteen inches long and as fat as silver dollars. So soup was possible after all. I felt sleepy all of a sudden and turned off the light.

Leek and potato soup. Leek and potato soup. The words were soothing now. Like white noise, sending me off to dreamland. All I had to do was order my seeds the next day. And get that potato order into Seeds Blum before they sold out of Urgentas and Ruby Crescents.

My eyes were riveted to the ceiling again. I hadn't even thought of that. What if the whole world had written to Boise, Idaho, before I did? Hadn't I missed out on Bintjes last year for that very same reason? What a sloth I was. I didn't deserve anything more than a supermarket spud, limp and chockful of pesticides. Hey, forget leeks. I'd drink instant onion soup. I needed more sodium.

I got up to fill out my potato order and spent the rest of the wee hours sorting through last year's seed packets. With enough seeds for two jillion plants, did I really need Chioggia, the heirloom beet with the red and white striped concentric circles? Yes. By dawn, I had all the envelopes sealed, the stamps on. By six, I was in one of those special post office lines for people with life-or-death business, sending out my seed orders, special delivery. By seven, I was home again, as rested as somebody just off the red-eye flight. So much for the relaxing, meditative joys of gardening. We type A personalities should stick to knitting. Something that isn't timed to the immutable seasons.

You can knit a ski sweater on the hottest day in August, and it'll still do its thing for you in February. While

Late Again

everybody's shivering in their chintzy machine-knit pullovers, you'll be warm and toasty in your Lope. But that won't work with a leek. Plant a leek too late and what've you got? Some little scallion as thin as a pencil, as flabby as celery left forgotten in the bottom of the fridge. A hopeless creature totally out of the running for potato and leek soup.

I envy those organized types who get all the seed discounts by ordering early. Who already have little shoots coming up in their greenhouses. Even while their gardens are as hard as rocks, as cold as glaciers. But I'm with Bob Thomson. He's a laid-back, relaxed gardener. And he's given me all the time in the world to plant those leeks. Or at least a couple of days.

Grass Roots

When I got my new Sears sprinkler hooked up, I felt at home for the first time since my quantum leap south. A week before, I'd been tending an obscure vegetable garden in Ipswich, Massachusetts. Now, I was suddenly Long Island's new Dan Rather of gardening (nightly wrap-ups on the hosta crisis and so on).

I was still shaky from the transplant. Labor-in-Vain Road had never been a good address for a writer or a gardener, but the Doll's House in Oyster Bay Cove seemed a near-schizophrenic plunge.

"Swish-swish-swish," my $13.99 Pulsator said.

This bothered me a little: I'd been looking for the kind that goes "thump-thump-thump, eh-eh-eh-eh." Either I'd gotten the wrong type of sprinkler, or I hadn't figured out the deep secret of the "easy-to-adjust trip collars," which were supposed to cut the circular watering pattern down to my pie-wedge piece of lawn.

Meanwhile, my little piece of sod was gasping, and I kept hearing the voice of Mario.

"You gotta water tonight," he had told me two days before as he laid the bathroom mats of green grass down in front of my cottage. (I'd decided to cheat a little and have an instant handkerchief lawn.) "If you don't water every day, the sod won't take root—and it'll die." I promised.

Mario, the landscaping wizard I'd found by word of mouth, has an Old World air of authority that sends me scrambling to follow his instructions. The Biancamano family didn't learn to shape the land at Harvard; a sense of design flows from their hands as naturally as a river rushes downstream. Mario and his father don't move rocks; they speak to them.

I could learn from these Earth men, but they don't hand out their secrets to just anybody. I promised to water. But because of a heavy workday, I couldn't get to the garden center for a hose even. By now, two afternoons later, those blades of grass looked as stiff as the needles on a fake Christmas tree.

I called my local extension service in a panic. Turf specialist Maria Cinque gave me a simple rundown on the basic types, but she could tell by my nervous "uh-huhs" (was that Mario's truck in the drive?) that I wasn't listening.

"Look," she said. Her voice was kind, patient; she was used to callers like me. "This isn't exactly a technical description, but I like the type that goes 'thump-thump-thump, eh-eh-eh-eh-eh.' "

Curiously enough, the man at Sears knew just what I was talking about. "Oh yeah," he said, cutting short my thump-thump-thump rendition. "Over there next to the oscillators . . ."

So I grabbed a Pulsator and ran home, only to spend the afternoon trying to fathom friction collars and regretting that I let my mechanical-genius boyfriend get away. Finally I flipped the little plastic whoozit that allowed for the full-circle swish-swish effect, and sat back to listen to the sod rug guzzle.

Let Mario drop by anytime. I was no lawn murderer.

Suddenly the world looked friendlier. I admired the two fat azaleas blooming on either side of my bare perennial bed.

"You should plant some nice daylilies in there," Mario had said. (He'd also suggested I find my dog, Molly, a boyfriend: "She's grouchy.") I'd wanted wildflowers, really, but my yard is all dappled shade. It would take me a while to get excited about hostas, which had always reminded me of funeral parlors. And doesn't bleeding heart sound like something that grows in the dark? These are morbid plants, but maybe there are cheerful shade lovers yet to be discovered.

I gave my Manalucie tomatoes a drink. The seedlings had journeyed down from Ipswich on top of a vacuum cleaner and a futon stuffed in the back of my Toyota. The gloriosa daisies, the zinnias and hollyhocks had made the trip in some old bread pans. Now everybody was happily making chloro-phyll on our new porch.

Dumb plants. Not a worry in the world, never even missed their mother. They didn't have to worry about where to buy a watering can, or if the county would give them a little building sand. They didn't sit around wondering where the Agway was—or if Long Island even had one.

I slunk off to the Long Island Nurserymen's Association dinner, using my Hagstrom's map to find Planting Fields Arboretum. The name suggested a big county-run farming operation, but everybody was wandering about in their evening clothes admiring barn-size copper beeches some king probably planted. Then we went into the castle for dinner.

I asked Jason Bailey, the man to my left, what kind of corn I should grow.

"You don't want to grow corn," he said, pouring more salt on his chicken cordon bleu.

"When you have some of Filasky's white corn in Brookville, you won't want to bother," Ruth DeSetta said.

But she didn't deny it was even better to have a plot near the kitchen so you could get the pot boiling before you picked the corn.

I mentioned my Manalucies. Now there's an old-fashioned variety that will grow into November, Bailey said. And you had to eat them, Ruth DeSetta said, with just a little extra-virgin olive oil and some fresh basil.

"No vinegar," warned Henry DeSetta. "The tomatoes have the acid."

We all nodded. Bailey folded his napkin and gave the new garden writer a little glance. "Hold off on that corn . . . maybe I can get you some seeds."

We settled back to hear a few stories about Jim Cross, the nurserymen's man of the year. The former stock consultant had bought some swamp out in Cutchogue years ago—and turned himself into a veritable Mendel of woody ornamentals.

Late that night I felt my way across my little triangle of grass. It squished reassuringly beneath my shoes, and I realized that swish-swish was just as good as thump-thump.

It's these little recognitions that turn a strange land into a home.

Dueling Trowels

*H*er dress was all wrong, painter Robert Dash declared from his side of the stage at the Parrish Art Museum.

Rosemary Verey stood very straight on *her* side of the stage in a long red dress, pearls and a brooch. Very proper, very English. The famous gardener had scrubbed her nails for two days.

But Dash, who does his gardening in Sagaponack, shook his head over the red dress.

"It's an inappropriate color," Dash grumbled, quite dazzling in his own white suit (and white sneakers newly purchased for the occasion). "It's inappropriate because *she's green*. Her hair is green, her face is green. She's totally *green*."

"But it's the only dress that doesn't crush in my suitcase," protested Verey, with the down-to-earth frankness of true nobility. But she took the dig for what it was, just another compliment from Dash, a Fellow of the Royal Horticultural

Society of London who'd dubbed himself a "green pipsqueak" compared with the "reigning queen of gardening."

This was the War of the Trowels. The Anglo-Saxon and the Yank were having a little gloves-off critique of each other's gardens to top off a day of garden tours and lectures recently sponsored by the Parrish Art Museum in Southampton.

We'd all tromped through Dash's garden that morning in a downpour that soaked our shoes but not our gardening spirits. The color, texture and proportion of the plants—trees, shrubs, vines, perennials, roses and vegetables—all growing in an unusual and eye-stopping harmony, are the natural outgrowth of an artist's soul.

"Look at that privet!" Verey had said, holding an old umbrella over her gray curls. "The way he *prunes* things." Dash's privet doesn't look like privet at all, at least not the dull, fat hedges Americans are used to. His is a tall, thin stand of gracefully sculpted limbs. "They look like dancing girls on a chorus line," said Verey, who was Dash's guest for the weekend.

We paused by a pot of leeks Dash had allowed to go to seed: they stood three feet high, with the long lines and bold curves of some abstract sculpture. "Only Robert would have thought of that," she said. "And look at those old oil jars by the bench. What a lovely place to sit."

We trailed after the others, Verey plucking off spent irises as we went. "I love how everything's lolling about," she said. "Every inch is covered. He uses his shrubs like coat hangers. Look at this clematis coming up through the holly."

It seemed so wonderfully abandoned, but it had an artist's sense of design. Somehow the drooping blooms of the columbine were more noticeable set against the asparagus, so tall and feathery one forgot it was a vegetable.

The curved, grassy path invited us to pause and gaze at every turn. "The paths, you see, are the bones of any garden," said Verey. "I love the way this is curved. It gives you a feeling of distance, of mystery; it invites you on."

Throughout the ebullient sparring that evening, it was clear the two gardeners agreed on one thing: Gardening is self-expression.

"Please remember that gardening is an art form, and unless you approach it that way, you might as well not do it at all," Dash said. "You have to experiment. The zing in a garden comes when you decide to break the rules. It's all in the act of the wrist—just like a painter."

The English had the basics down all right, said the painter, but his tone suggested they could let themselves go a bit: "The English have two ideas. Manure, manure, manure. And prune, prune, prune. They say you should prune a bush until you can stick your head through."

Verey rolled her eyes heavenward, as if thinking of England. "No, Robert, it's so a bird can *fly* through."

Any gardener unfamiliar with Verey's work is in for a treat. The best of her many books, *Classic Garden Design* and *The Scented Garden*, are not only filled with countless ideas and how-tos but her delightful references to early garden literature also serve as a kind of joyful syllabus for self-education.

That night, the dueling trowels showed slides of their gardens:

"*She* has gardeners to do all that; *I'm* the whole show," Dash grumbled, as Verey's knot garden appeared on the screen. Verey said nothing; Dash was just jealous. We can't grow boxwood so lush here (though *Classic Garden Design* will tell you how the British do it).

Besides, on other occasions her fingernails have proved

otherwise. "I think the English have a heartier attitude toward gardening," she had said earlier that day. "They're not afraid to get down there and *dig*."

Verey's very first crop was some "not very salubrious" carrots she planted at the age of ten. Since then, she's grown more sophisticated: laying the brick for a patterned vegetable garden inspired by the garden at the Château de Villandry on the Loire, planting an apple-tree tunnel after she saw the one at Tyningham in Scotland. But to an Englishwoman of Verey's ilk, gardening is as natural as breathing.

"I can't understand how someone can't tell an annual from a biennial, can you?" she said. "To me, it's like brushing your teeth. You just know, subconsciously."

A slide of Barnsley House, Verey's English manor house, appeared on one side of the screen: fourteenth-century stone, with a wide lawn mown in sweeps that make it look striped and plenty of clipped yews. *Ooh*, the audience breathed.

Dash's low-slung colonial cottage and riotous landscape appeared on the other half of the screen. The colors and textures of the garden had a delightful sense of abandonment, boldly accented by a bright blue door. *Ah*, the audience sighed.

"Ha-hah!" shouted Dash, thinking he was pulling ahead.

"I'm very attached to that blue Robert has put on his door," Verey admitted, ever gracious. "Mine is more conventional. Look at my stripy lawn."

Dash agreed, mirthfully *un*gracious. "No, I wouldn't mow a lawn that way. Do you *like* those clipped yews?"

Verey looked a bit taken aback. "Well . . . we *have* to clip them. They're too high . . . I like the formality of it." Then she mentioned maybe she'd put in a moat—to keep unwanted American visitors away.

Next on the screen, the Etruscan temple Verey's husband gave her more than twenty years ago. "For a long time there was no center point in my garden," she said. "It wasn't until the temple was moved in that I had a focal point."

"No one ever gave *me* a temple," said Dash.

"Well," said Verey, who used to ride to hounds, "perhaps you haven't applied to the right person."

Dash suggested she get a resident hermit to live in her temple.

And so it went, Verey chatting as casually about the great gardens of the world as if she'd grown up in them; Dash exhorting us to take up those pruning shears and be bold, original.

"One must never be afraid to copy," Verey said quietly. "After I saw the Château de Villandry, I came home with this nagging urge to get *on* with it." And not only did Verey's vegetable garden have Villandry's geometric patterns, it also had the borders of herbs and roses and lavender she'd discovered by reading the seventeenth-century garden notes of William Lawson.

"You must always carry a notebook and pencil," she said. "Otherwise, you'll be constantly asking yourself, 'What was that wonderful idea I had this morning . . . ?' "

But it was the slide of Verey's laburnum walk that silenced the green pipsqueak from Sagaponack.

"I'm not commenting—because I'm so *consumed* by jealousy," Dash admitted. We'd wandered through *his* laburnum walk that morning.

Verey just smiled, admiring her own work.

"Well, I take Robert's laburnum walk as a compliment," she said. "Mine is a bit older than his, so I think he copied mine."

Ancient Trees

A long time ago, the gods used to pay occasional visits to earth, just to test people.

Remember when Jupiter and Mercury were so tired and hungry, and everybody turned them away except for Baucis and Philemon? These two made a fire in their humble hearth, pulled a few carrots from the garden, wiped off the table with some fresh mint (Baucis had to stick a tile under the fourth leg to keep it from tilting) and served up a simple, tasty dinner, complete with wine. (Ovid says the wine was "of no great age," which makes me think it was probably a hearty Burgundy, perhaps Gallo.)

To make a long story short, after making pigs of themselves, the gods asked their hosts to make a wish. And Baucis and Philemon—the two old lovebirds that they were—asked that when it was time to die, they both go at the same instant.

"Done," said Jupiter, folding his napkin. Then he destroyed the whole village (for being rude), set up Baucis and Philemon as caretakers in his temple—and years later, at some appropriate moment, turned them both into trees. What once were two loving bodies could now grow into eternity—together.

We've forgotten these old stories about trees—because the great big ones, the ones that look like the bodies of the gods themselves, all twisted and gnarled with great strong trunks and branches like burly arms and legs—are slowly disappearing. No one has room in the yard for an enormous copper beech, or a linden or an oak. We're lucky to squeeze in a little Japanese maple out back. And besides, every seven years everybody moves to California, or at least to another town on Long Island. Who has time to watch something big grow?

But we need such largeness—for our imaginations, and our sense of eternity. We need to remember our own myths, to keep a little mystery in our lives. Gordon Jones, the director of the Planting Fields Arboretum on the old Coe estate in Oyster Bay, says he took his job "for the trees."

The young horticulturist first drove onto the Island thirty years ago for his interview. It was a hot, sticky August afternoon, and Jones felt terribly uneasy.

"To a rural upstater the Island was overwhelming . . . all the traffic and people," he recalls. But then I turned onto Wolver Hollow, and then Chicken Valley Road and finally the Planting Fields. And I had this incredible feeling—of not being a stranger here. It was the trees."

Jones walked about alone for a few minutes, just to calm himself before his interview. He looked at the beeches, and the giant lindens, the oaks and elms, the weeping hemlock.

And he decided to spend a lifetime here—watching over the old trees and planting hundreds of new ones.

"Every day I go out and there's just a special feeling because of the trees," he says. "They lend something of majesty and a quiet peace to the place."

Jones showed me a few of his favorites: the Sargent weeping hemlock that rests on the grass like some great Medusa head, the silver linden whose flowers make the bees so drunk they lie stunned on the ground, the old purple beech whose trunk has the ancient look of elephant skin. Its branches look like old knees, stomachs with stretch marks.

"Children run toward that one," Jones says with a little smile. (And though it's forbidden to climb, you get the feeling Jones sometimes turns his head if the child is young enough.)

This is the beech that was moved 160 miles across the sea on a barge from Fairhaven, Massachusetts, to Oyster Bay in the late winter of 1915. The young Mrs. Coe—the daughter of Henry Huttleson Rogers—had grown lonely for the tree she'd played beneath as a child, and her husband, William, moved it—for $4,000.

Jones tells me about the trees he's lost.

"They do die, you know," he says. "Finally you have to say, 'It's time' ... rather than letting them agonize like old people in a nursing home."

He raises his arms in a little gesture of how difficult all this is to put into words. This courtly man looks tiny in his venerable old plant world.

"The largest, most majestic of all—a giant silver linden that must have been a hundred years old—went over in a mini-tornado that blew up one afternoon about ten years ago," he says. The northeast wind was gone within minutes—but it toppled the ninety-footer, ripping its massive stump and roots clear out of the ground.

When I ask Jones how he felt, he just shakes his head. No words.

My grandmother planted maples in front of her husband's house soon after she left her mother's home at the age of sixteen. She grew old with these trees and taught us about the birds that sang in them. My mother watched the sun rise every morning through the branches of her willow tree. She was an Eastern Shore girl, and maybe the marsh-loving tree reminded her of the home she had left behind. I have no trees like this in my new home—so I go to the Planting Fields.

At dawn, it's dark beneath the Sargent weeping hemlock, and quiet as the word "primeval." Somewhere outside, crows are calling to one another, but under this dense canopy, it is perfectly still.

One thick branch has crossed over to join and grow into another, and it's hard to tell beginning from end. Other branches have leaned so far down to the ground, they've taken root, grown back upward, and formed new trunks and branches of their own. Everything about this old tree is circular, wavy, as if some ancient water current had shaped it.

As the crow flies, the Planting Fields Arboretum isn't far from the Long Island Expressway, but it feels like another country. You can forget the roads jammed with cars, the Dunkin' Donuts, the McDonald's, the Hot Bagel shops already filled with long, impatient lines. Here, at the arboretum, it's easy to remember that trees were once the homes of gods.

Bird Consciousness

*I*t was my grandmother who introduced me to birds. We'd rock on the front porch, in the deep afternoon, taking in the cool breeze blowing through the maples, talking in that meandering way that has no goal in mind.

"Is that Frank down by the hedgerow? He was up again this morning, standing at the screen door, asking me to pray with him. He better start praying over that tractor, now . . ." Her hands would never stop on the endless afghans she crocheted. She must have made miles of them.

Then she'd ssssh! herself, and say, "Hear that? Do you know what bird that is?" And I'd have to guess robin, or bobwhite or catbird, or blue jay, and then we'd get on with our lazy passing of the afternoon. Nothing ever happened and we liked it that way. And I never thought much about the birds. We had a pet crow with a broken wing, which my brother had found in the A & P parking lot. It lived with the chickens and sat in the window of the coop, saying, "Hello!" but that was about it. Birds were just part of the landscape, like Frank trying to give us religion, and the potato rolls Grandmother baked on Saturdays.

But now that I live on a marsh, fed by a river that rises and falls with the tides, I am interested in birds, as individuals. The first night in my cottage, an owl kept me awake. I was used to city noises. In the morning, a pair of red-winged blackbirds flitted among the cattails. Two cardinals have stayed the winter, and a noisy, ring-necked pheasant.

But it wasn't until I borrowed a friend's binoculars, a few weeks ago, that I began to realize birds have stepped, on careful feet, into my consciousness. It was one of those unseasonably warm mornings, with no wind, and a blue sky. The marsh grass was a golden brown, and the tide was going out. I focused the glasses on a line of mallards and a few black ducks, drifting down the river, and then scanned the opposite shore. I was struck by the illogical effect of the glasses, which not only focus the eyes on a narrow slice of the usually 180-degree landscape, but seem to silence that world as well. Which is an illusion, of course, but it has to do with the sudden telescoping of reality.

What was an unidentifiable blob to my naked eye, shimmering a hundred yards out on the flats, suddenly jumped into focus with my eight-powered lenses. It was a yellow-crowned night heron standing motionless on a log. I could actually see the yellow feathers on the top of his head, the sliver of white on his black face, and he had no idea that I was looking at him.

There's an almost voyeuristic thrill to bird-watching, of watching something that doesn't know it's being watched. This heron was acting in the perfectly natural way we all do when we assume we're alone. And I felt I was in on something almost surreptitious.

I think that's where the illusion of silence comes from. The mind blocks out what the ear is hearing, because the mind's ear is trained out there, a hundred yards away. And since the glasses can't focus sound, the mind registers silence. Which increases that sense of distilled experience, as if one is sitting in a darkened theater and actually stepping into the larger-than-life, impossibly beautiful story on the screen. You forget that you're looking at it. You almost feel as if you *are* it. And you certainly don't hear the person crunching popcorn next to you. That's the pleasure, I'm discovering, of watching birds with a high-powered lens. The very birdness of the bird is concentrated.

So those lonely looking souls out there, the tall, skinny men, the stout ladies in hats, whom I've so long assumed to be oddballs, eggheads, anal compulsive list-makers, are actually experiencing what in the sixties might have been associated with an acid trip. An out-of-body experience. For an instant, we bird-watchers are no longer standing in a wet marsh, feeling the icy brine seep into our tennis shoes; we're standing on long yellow legs, waiting for some crab to scuttle across the flat.

Once you've had this experience with your first bird, it's a little bit like Helen Keller standing with her hands under the water pump, struggling to form the word "wahhhh-terrrr." Hundreds of bird questions come tumbling into your mind. You want to focus on all the other birds out there, formerly just ho-hum ducks and herons. What makes one different from another? What is a scaup, anyway, other than the last word to the crossword puzzle?

This naming business is an interesting thing in itself.

Why, that is, we humans are driven to name everything. Is it our egos? Some kind of narcissistic belief that by naming a creature we possess it? I don't think so. I think it has more to do with our immersion, over the millennia, in language. Until we have a word for something, it hardly exists, except in some vague blurry way that is as unfocused and dreamy as the distant shore without a pair of binoculars. It's beautiful, and pleasant, and we'd miss it if it disappeared, but it hasn't entered our consciousness in a specific, satisfying way.

The beauty of winter bird-watching is similar to any other passion that brings you out of the stuffy, overheated house and into a landscape that others assume to be frozen and dead until the crocuses pop up. There's a bit of the pleasure of having a secret, of hoping the whole world stays inside, in exploring a deserted beach along Oyster Bay Cove, or Setauket Harbor, or the Jamaica Bay Wildlife Refuge, and spotting the chestnut red head and swooping black bill of a male canvasback duck. Or recognizing a bufflehead simply by the way he flies out of the water, his small size and velvety black head, with its startling patch of white.

And through the glasses, time stops. You watch the yellow-crowned night heron lift that yellow leg slowly, slowly, slowly. And then just put it down. Or the burst of light from water as he snaps up a tiny minnow. But there's no sense of waiting, impatiently, for something to happen. He simply stands there, motionless, in the morning, doing nothing.

The Year of
One Tomato

*O*nce upon a time, way back in 1987, it was the Year of the Tomato. This decree came not from the President—he was too busy trying to remember, or trying to forget, about other things that year—but rather from the National Garden Bureau, an organization in Willowbrook, Illinois, funded by the U.S. seed industry.

Each year, the NGB elevated some popular vegetable that almost any nincompoop could grow, in hopes of selling new and wonderful seeds (1986 had been the Year of Corn), and firing the spirit of home gardeners throughout the land. No doubt the NGB hoped to instill some feeling in gardeners that they were a part not only of nature's own grand plan, but of some vast geopolitical order as well.

And as often happens in such cases, those individuals who should have been most honored were lost in the shuffle of the glory-seekers.

"We developed the subarctic tomato!" shouted one seed company.

"We developed Tiny Tim!" shouted another.

Meanwhile, the tomatoes, totally ignorant that this was *their* year, continued to grow. One such tomato, a Sweet 100 Hybrid, will be remembered here today, in honor of all the unknown tomatoes of 1987 that grew their little hearts out that summer without ever giving their existence, or its importance, a single thought.

This particular Sweet 100—a humble cherry tomato— grew from a seed that was one of 800,000 or so sold that year by the Park Seed Company of Greenwood, South Carolina. Its ancestors hailed from Peru, but its parents may have grown up in Taiwan.

"The parents would have had to be hand-pollinated, and that means finding cheap labor in some Third World country," said George B. Park, the grandson of George W. Park, who founded the company about 120 years before this Sweet 100 first saw the light of day. "That Sweet 100's parents may have been grown near Taiwan, which has a good climate for the tomato—lots of sun and not too much fluctuation in temperature." And plenty of peasants.

It's probable, then, that some nonunion worker picked the pollen off the Sweet 100's female parent to keep it from pollinating itself, then took pollen from the male parent and rubbed it onto the pistil of the female's flower. If all went well, and no revolution or hailstorm rocked the field, the tomatoes ripened and were picked. Their seeds were dried in the sun and sent to the Park Seed Company, where they were tested for germination and varietal purity, to make sure some bee hadn't flown into the Taiwan field and crossed the wrong things up.

Here our particular seed enjoyed a temperature-and-humidity-controlled room and a ride in the spiral bowl feeder, which sent it and twenty-nine other seeds into a gold-foil Parkspak.

This Parkspak, "sealed at scientifically controlled low-moisture content to insure peak vigor in the seed until you are ready to plant," was put in a UPS truck sometime in February, and transported from South Carolina to Oyster Bay, New York.

No doubt, on that cold, windy day, it rolled by spectacular scenery: the sun popping up over the Blue Ridge Mountains and setting over the golden arches of one of those hamburger chains so popular back in 1987.

But did our little tomato seed give a hoot? Of course not. It had no eyes to see, no nose to sniff. Even if it had, our seed was sealed off from the sensual world by the scientifically controlled Parkspak.

But not for long. The truck pulled up to a snow-covered cottage, and the driver stumbled down the icy path. An unscientifically controlled dog stuck her head out the dog door and barked at the man. (In 1987, dog brains had not evolved enough to discern a UPS person from a thief.)

The box containing our seed was left on the ramshackle porch, where it was buffeted by February winds, until a little girl came by to feed the unevolved dog. (The gardener who had ordered this seed was, as fate would have it, in Peru. But our Sweet 100 wasn't interested in its ancestors; it was getting cold out on the porch.)

The little girl was sensible enough to bring in the box of

seeds, whereupon the dog sat on it whilst waiting for her kibble, creating another fluctuation in temperature.

Enter the gardener, finally returned from her long journey, who opened the box in a wave of the maniacal enthusiasm felt by her kind in mid-March. Then she started playing back her answering machine and left the Parkspak to bake beneath a 100-watt bulb.

Fate is cruel. Our seed could have arrived at the home of an orderly gardener, who would have placed the gold-foil packet in the fridge until time for planting in a soft moist bed of potting soil. She would have covered it with vermiculite and sphagnum moss, and a sheet of cellophane to keep it moist. She would have laid it on heating coils that never dropped below 70 degrees.

But what happened? Real life, that's what. Like the gardener drinking beer at the very moment the seedbed dried out. Like a heating coil that didn't work, and a greenhouse window that broke when the wind came up and sent the branch of a black walnut tree crashing to the roof. More fluctuations in temperature.

Many Sweet 100 seeds died that night. But *our* seed went on to germinate, and when it developed its first true leaves, it was gently placed in a little pot, where it began to develop into a strong, sturdy plant.

No, wait a minute. That's a fairy tale. It should have been placed in a little pot, but it was kept too long in the seedbed, until its roots became entangled with others. It was allowed to fry in the hot midday sun and shiver in the cold nights of the unscientific greenhouse. It wilted from lack of water and almost drowned in too much. Its stem grew leggy, its leaves kind of yellow.

Such was life in Oyster Bay. When our Sweet 100 was finally planted in mid-May, it wilted in the sun of high noon, then shivered in a cold snap that suddenly hit the area. Then it got warm. Then it got cold. Warm, cold. Dry, wet, dry again.

The Year of the Tomato was not a great year for the tomato. A Tiny Tim was downed by a cutworm. A Beefsteak developed leaf roll. Many succumbed to whiteflies. An Early Girl produced early, and her fruit began to girlishly blush, when a raccoon had his way with her. A subarctic turned red, but it tasted like a tomato ripened in an icebox.

And our Sweet 100? As rock-solid as the Andes, as enduring as the Aztecs, she took her own good sweet time getting ripe. But finally those perfect little green balls turned red.

Now did the gardener fall to her knees at this miraculous occurrence? Did she worship this humble, sturdy plant before stuffing her mouth with those sweet red cherries?

No. She thought how nice it was to be bending over her warm tomato patch, its peppery aroma filling her hair, gobbling down Sweet 100s, as fast as she possibly could.

She's a Cucuza

*L*ouis Boccia refers to his favorite plant as *her.* And he's reported on *her* progress all summer long.

"She's up to the roof of the garage now."

"She's climbed clear *over* the roof now."

"She's gone across the yard and into the tree."

Finally, the press arrived.

Boccia led the way into his tiny backyard in Valley Stream and stared up at *her* as she just sat, or lay, or basked, or grew, really, on an ingenious trellis that her keeper, a sixty-seven-year-old retired meat cutter, keeps extending as she gets bigger and bigger.

We stared up at the leaves, as big as frying pans, and the pendulous fruit—almost a dozen pale green squashes, each the size of a baseball bat—hanging straight down from the sturdy vines.

"How do you know she's a her?"

"Well, look at her," Boccia's wife, Louise, said, giggling. "It's just common sense. No *he* could produce those." We stared at the great long squashes in silence. We giggled joyfully, like adolescents in a sex-education class.

"Boy, you could really defend yourself with one of those bats, huh?" Louise Boccia said.

Its skin is a lovely green, smooth and covered with a fine fuzz. "That protects the squash from insects," said Boccia proudly, as if his pet had every angle covered.

Boccia started *her* from seed, taken from her grandmother's firstborn last summer.

"They say the seed from the first squash is the best," said Boccia, passing on a bit of folk wisdom from the ancient past.

He started the seed in a peat pot in late March and set the young plant out this past spring, two weeks after Mother's Day.

"Just dug a hole, threw in a little 5-10-5 with some cow manure, buried her about an inch or so, covered her up and let her grow," said Boccia.

Well, he did give her a couple of shots of Miracle-Gro the first month and a half, and his daughter, Josephine, complained that she couldn't take a shower some nights because Dad was out there watering the squash. She doesn't complain too much, though. "It's the only squash I like to eat," said Josephine.

Boccia's horticultural feat is the perfect example of the principle that less is more. Would a single zucchini seed, showered with the same love and attention, grow over the house? Could one sunflower, treated with such tenderness, stick its face through the clouds?

The Boccias beamed at the maternal squash plant with all the affection and pride others might bestow on a beloved pig that's just given birth to a prizewinning litter.

"Can you believe this? One plant," said Boccia.

She begins—a stem about the diameter of a quarter—on one side of the yard, climbs up a wire leading to the garage, travels over a roof (where she's elevated two feet above the tar shingles to keep her cool), weaves her way across a trapezelike contraption made of rubber wire and wood and is happily strangling a little tree about twenty yards from her point of origin.

"I think that tree's dying," said Boccia. But his worried tone was for the squash. "What'll I grow her on if that thing goes?"

The Boccias told how they brought everything inside last year before Hurricane Gloria blew through the yard—everything, that is, but her grandmother.

"Afterward, she was still there," said Louise Boccia. "Nothing can take one of these down."

"Except a good hard frost," said Boccia. "But I'm kind of glad it doesn't stay warm year-round. I don't know where she'd end up!"

The Boccias aren't even sure of the variety of this grande dame of squashes. They call it green summer squash, or Sicilian squash.

And they love to eat the squash almost as much as they love to watch *her* grow.

"A lot of work, though, let me tell you," said Louise Boccia. "All that peeling, and the seeds and the pulp. Whew. After all that, I get tired."

"What's the flavor like?"

"Flavor?" Boccia echoed. "Not much flavor. The flavor is what you flavor it *with*." With that, he picked one of his squash babies, and Louise Boccia gave me a couple of recipes. I trotted home with my green baseball bat.

The reactions along the way were interesting: Some

averted their eyes in genteel embarrassment. Others greeted the sight like some memory from the old country.

"Ah, the gu-gu-za!" said one. "My grandmother used to stuff them!"

"Oh, a cu-cu-za!" said another. "Some people hollow them out and *play* them." He grabbed the squash and bonged it with an imaginary drumstick. Whatever it is, it inspires affection. Why is the interesting question.

I had some difficulty getting my squash through the front door. It weighed in on the bathroom scale at five pounds. It was forty inches long. It rolled off my cutting board. I got out Louise Boccia's recipes and set to.

She was right. This squash is a lot of work. And I'm not so sure it's worth it. My first experiment was with the squash pie—your basic quiche with peeled, deseeded and chopped "cucuza," instead of zucchini or crab, or what have you, as the extra ingredient. It was delicious—thanks to all those eggs and the nice tangy Locatelli cheese. But as far as I could tell, the Sicilian squash—as the Boccias had told me—had no flavor.

On to the stuffed idea. This was fun. You peel part of the baseball bat (one squash makes several recipes) into 2½-inch rings, hollow them out and stuff them with a meatball-type mixture. (Louise Boccia uses chopped meat, bread crumbs, eggs, garlic, fresh parsley, salt and pepper to taste.) Then you simmer it in a homemade tomato sauce—with plenty of fresh basil. Now what wouldn't be delicious stuffed and smothered with such yummy ingredients?

Again, the dish was delicious—but the squash had nothing to do with it. (Actually, I've been thinking those hollow rings dried would make great napkin rings.)

What, then, accounts for this squash's magnificent place accorded in the Boccia backyard—and kitchen?

Well, if you saw a "cucuza" growing, you'd understand. There's something mysterious and wonderful—and well, incredibly *fertile* about the Sicilian squash. And I contend that this plant has a sense of humor. How else could it expose itself in such a nonchalant, easygoing manner? Just dangling there, unaffected by giggles or the questions of children.

They say squash grew in the hanging gardens of Babylon. Surely, it was one of *her* ancestors.

Overkill

One morning in late May, my neighbor strolled out across her field and noticed that her pine trees looked sickly. She got a little closer and saw that tiny worms were feeding on the needles and that many of the branches were as bare as dead sticks.

The worms were the larvae of pine sawflies, but she didn't know that. She didn't even know that these were pine trees. To her, they were just lovely old evergreens that she didn't want to lose.

So she went to Flowertime and bought a bottle of some chemical—she doesn't remember its name and she's since thrown it away—whose label said it would kill the insects. She spritzed the yellowish dust on the smaller trees, but realized that much of it was drifting down into her face. She also decided the exercise was futile because her trees are well over a hundred feet tall.

Overkill

My neighbor isn't the type to sit around and do nothing. So after asking her cooperative extension agent for advice, she turned to the Yellow Pages and called a tree sprayer certified in pesticide application. The truck arrived in short order.

"It looked like a utility company truck, only mounted on the roof was a chair and a barrel the shape of a cement mixer," my neighbor said. "A man sat on top dressed in what looked like outer-space gear and goggles." She described how the man could aim the pesticide spray—which had the force of a fire hose—by turning a steering wheel attached to the mixer.

The company had advised the family to evacuate during the spraying, so they locked their cat in the house and got in the car. But before they left, they watched the truck make a complete loop around the field that fronts their house.

The pesticide, methoxychlor, worked. The pine sawflies died. But so did the goldfish in a little wading pool beneath the wisteria arbor beside the house. Three weeks after the trees were sprayed, an oily film appeared on the surface of the pond and the fish—about thirty or so—all floated to the top, belly up.

Now, this could have just been some kind of bizarre coincidence. And, unfortunately, my neighbor drained the pond and disposed of the fish—without having either water or fish chemically analyzed. Who would have? Murder wasn't committed. It was just a case of a homeowner trying to save her trees.

But she wondered about the possible connection. These goldfish were hardy creatures. They'd survived three winters. She could think of nothing unusual that had happened over those three weeks—except the chemical spraying.

I called half a dozen pesticide experts. I felt sad about the fish. And frustrated about my compost pile, which I'd spent a year building. My neighbor's husband trimmed the wisteria and threw the vines on the pile—then remembered about the spraying. So now we had to assume the old one was contaminated, and start a new one.

Methoxychlor is a widely used organochlorine, a member of the DDT family, I learned from the National Resources Defense Council. The pesticide is one tenth as toxic as DDT, and it breaks down more quickly, but it's more persistent than an organophosphate. Organophosphates, favored because they biodegrade quickly, are acutely toxic—Mexican farmworkers tending vegetables for the U.S. market have died from these sprays. We're just talking about a few fish.

"Methoxychlor is moderately toxic to fish, but if there's an acute exposure, the fish usually die quickly, within ninety-six hours," said Ell-Piret Multer, at the National Fishery Research Laboratory in Columbia, Missouri. "I'm afraid nobody will ever know what happened to those fish, unless the tissue itself is analyzed. Maybe they died of oxygen depletion or some disease. It could be terribly coincidental—unless an excess amount somehow got into the pond. That's within the realm of possibility." Maybe it drifted on the wind. Maybe it washed off the leaves. Maybe it had nothing to do with their death.

They could have starved to death, said Leonard Flynn, a consultant to the American Council on Science. Flynn, who has a Ph.D. in chemistry and is a certified pest-control operator, has just finished a booklet for the council, titled *Pesticides: Do We Really Need Them?*

"Organochlorines are relatively persistent, and when an

area is sprayed, the insecticide doesn't just kill the sawflies. It kills aquatic insects and spiders as well. Possibly, their food supply was destroyed," he said. "Though that's pure supposition."

Flynn explained that organochlorines and organophosphates both kill insects by interfering with an enzyme called cholinesterase, which is necessary for nerve transmission. "Both pesticides inhibit cholinesterase from doing its job, which means the nerve transmissions get jammed up and the organism is paralyzed," he said. "If humans took a lethal dose, it would be the same situation."

And there's another problem here. "Organochlorines are very persistent. Most have been banned in this country because of environmental contamination. They tend to be fat-soluble and they concentrate in the food chain," said Michael Hansen, an agricultural ecologist at the Institute for Consumer Policy Research in Mount Vernon, New York.

Hansen recalled a case in California. In 1949, a lake was sprayed with DDT to rid it of gnats. Five years later, all the grebes on the lake died.

"The levels of DDT found in their blood were 100,000 times greater than the levels in the lake," said Hansen. Over the years, the lake's microscopic organisms had filtered the water, absorbed the chemical and passed it up the food chain. With every link, the pesticide grew more concentrated.

Though far less toxic and less persistent than DDT, methoxychlor has the same problem of bioaccumulation, Hansen told me.

What if the pine sawflies come back? Will my neighbor spray again? She says she'd certainly do more research this time to try to find some alternative. She tells me how she found the pesticide label tucked in between receipts for a donation to Earthwatch and one to the Cold Spring Harbor Fish Hatchery. My neighbor cares about these things.

Maybe there was an alternative she could have pursued. One entomologist suggested a dormant oil spray. Another said that wouldn't work. One expert said the trees could have survived the damage; another said they would have died. A cooperative extension agent told me methoxychlor was an organophosphate, a fairly major bit of misinformation.

With all these contradictions and out-and-out errors flying around, how can anyone make a wise decision?

Even if properly applied, methoxychlor has a residual effect, so it adds to the contamination of the planet. But if your favorite trees are threatened, will you use the pesticide, just a little, anyway? I think this is the question of the century, and one that gardeners, as tenders of the earth, must ask.

Answering the Call

This is how gardening by telephone starts: a little pink "While You Were Out" slip with a name and number.

Sometimes, there's a message.

"Mrs. McDonough's husband has some unusually large tomatoes."

Sometimes it's one cryptic word: "Pineapple."

Or just a scrap of white paper some phantom leaves on my desk: "Joe Torre—175-pound pumpkin."

One pink slip from a Mr. Migbella has the "urgent" box checked off.

I call: "Is Mr. Migbella in?"

"Who?" a voice shouts.

"Uh, maybe I have the name wrong. Somebody called *Newsday* about a gardening matter."

"Ohhhhh! Yeahhhh! The name's De-*Bel*-la! Hey, Dad!" his wife says. "It's the girl from *Newsday*!"

Dad gets on the phone. "Hey-*low*? Yeah, I got this thing in my garden, and I don't know what it is. I think a bird planted it—but where did he get the seed? At first it looked kinda like a dandelion but now it's over my head! I'm eighty-four years old and I've never seen anything like this."

Mr. DeBella's voice expresses a wonderful awe, and I tell him I'll try to get out there as soon as I can.

The phone rings as soon as I hang up.

"Hello? This is Mrs. Porter. I have what's supposed to be a whaddyacallit, a zucchini, but it's more like a giant bat with a melon on one end, and it's got a meat that's a cantaloupe color. I think the bees took over and cross-pollinated it!"

I promise I'll get right out there.

"Bring your camera!" Mrs. Porter shouts. "Maybe we've invented something! Maybe we can sell it to a seed company. 'The Porters' Zucchini-Melon-Cousin!' " Or a Squelon, I say, but she's hung up.

The 175-pound phantom pumpkin has found its way to an Italian bakery somewhere in Lindenhurst. Nobody seems to speak English, and I start to shout like the worst kind of American tourist. A young woman is called to the phone. She sounds quite irritated.

"It's a big pumpkin. In the window. The owner grew it." Can you give me directions? "Busy Bee Mall. On Wellwood Ave. We close at five."

Now you probably think we garden writers drift about picking flowers and talking to vegetables (as Prince Charles does). When the fall wind blows, we retire to our little cottages, to sip chamomile tea and design next spring's herbal knot garden.

How I wish. In real life, we're out on the road with our

Hagstrom maps, trying to find little teensy-weensy dead-end streets in Plainview or Elwood, or Northport, or West Hempstead. We're fighting traffic jams in front of malls the first day of back-to-school sales, while never-to-be-seen-again plants quietly reach their peak.

"Hey-*low?*" It's Mr. DeBella again. "You said you were coming out here. My weed is still growing."

Time waits for no man, and neither will a weed for a garden writer. I got in my car and drove.

Peter DeBella had his sports jacket on when I arrived, and he stood beneath his giant weed with an air of Old World dignity.

"Look," I said. "It's blooming."

"Wha?" DeBella stood back, the better to see his weed. Some nondescript little puffballs were sitting up there like spent dandelions atop the Empire State Building.

"Whaddyaknow. I didn't even notice," he said. He snapped off one of the leaves, shaped like those of a dandelion, only bigger. He broke off a stem, which "bled" just like a milk-weed plant.

We hemmed and hawed over the mystery. This was one for the New York Botanical Garden. Next day, I presented a leaf, kept overnight in a Baggie in my fridge, to Joseph Beitel, a top scientist at the garden.

"Oh, that's a compass plant!" said Beitel. "Member of the composite family. The leaves are supposed to turn north and south. The daisy . . . lettuce . . . they're all part of the same family."

DeBella was going to love this. Beitel had sought out plants as far-flung as the rain forest of Cerro de la Neblina, a 10,000-foot-high mountain east of the Andes. And now, he'd given our humble weed its name.

Next morning, bright and early, Mr. DeBella's on the line: "Well?"

I quote Beitel. I read him the section on the composite family in my *Wyman's Gardening Encyclopedia.*

But DeBella sounds disgusted when I read that the compass plant, *Silphium laciniatum*, has a large and showy flower.

"My plant has a *little white* bloom," he says with a weary sigh, as if some other person should have my job.

"Could you put my plant in the paper? Maybe somebody [who knows something] will see it and know what it is!"

Dear reader, name this plant.

But before I sign off, a few more items from the International Plant Desk:

Rita Muller grows pineapples by twisting the tops off the ones she buys in the A & P. Sam Maratto's Super Belgian Giant tomato plant was fourteen feet high when it last posed for *Newsday*. Charles Lucania's cucuza weighs seventeen pounds.

"Are you sure?" Lucania said as I stood on the bathroom scale in his yard holding the fifty-five-inch squash. "I thought sure it would be about thirty . . ."

And about Joe Torre's 175-pound pumpkin, now on exhibit at Santa's Bakery in north Lindenhurst: It looks more like some kind of mutant winter squash to me, sitting among all those delicate little pastries, but what do I know? I can't even identify a weed. If anybody can, I'm here, waiting, by the phone.

The Dirt on
Earthworms

A little girl asked me a long time ago what happens to the earthworms in the winter. An interesting question, which I sort of forgot about until the winds started howling, and I found out that neither God nor my landlord plows my driveway after a snowstorm.

Too bad earthworms don't plow snow the way they plow the earth, I thought, as I found a rusty, bent shovel in the garage and started acting like somebody out of *O Pioneers!* My lower back began to complain, and I considered calling my local gas station, whose owner plows for a small fortune.

Earthworms have it good in weather like this: curled up into little balls, way down at the bottom of their burrows, just beneath the frost line, waiting for the thaw. Lucky them. Nobody expects anything from an earthworm this time of year. Nobody's on the phone, saying, "When do you think you'll make it in to work?"

But I don't begrudge them their time off. After all, they're out there from early spring to late fall, churning old rotten leaves into rich, dark humus. Without the humble earthworm, we'd be hefting our pickaxes against hard-packed ground, as airless, dry and dead as concrete. But thanks to our wriggly, slimy little friends, we sift our fingers through black gold. And when we put out those first cabbage plants in early spring, their tender roots will take hold in the humus-lined burrows of the earthworms. How nice of them.

My botany textbook, *Biology of Plants*, mentions that the manure, or castings, of an earthworm contains five times the nitrogen of surrounding soil, seven times the phosphorus, eleven times the potassium, three times the magnesium and two times the calcium. One teaspoon of soil, duly enriched by earthworms, can contain as many as 5 billion bacteria, 20 million fungi, 1 million protozoa. So next time you say "Ick" upon meeting a worm, say "Thank you" instead.

Charles Darwin, who studied earthworms for more than forty years, loved these ignominious animals: "The plough is one of the most ancient and most valuable of man's inventions," he wrote, "but long before he existed the land was in fact regularly ploughed, and still continues to be thus ploughed by earthworms. It may be doubted whether there are many other animals which have played so important a part in the history of the world, as have these lowly, organized creatures."

Aristotle called earthworms the "intestines of the earth," and he was absolutely right. The earthworm is barely more than a digestive tract, with just enough of a brain to shovel food in one end and send nitrogen-rich humus out the other. But even an earthworm has tastes, Darwin said. His earthworms showed a decided preference for celery, cabbage and carrots; they disliked sage, thyme, mint and other spicy foods. But then these earthworms were British.

Anyway, Darwin credited the earthworm with depositing soft, fluffy topsoil on top of everything from Roman bathhouses to the stones at Stonehenge to his own rocky field:

"For several years it was clothed with an extremely scant vegetation, and was so thickly covered with small and large flints (some of them half as large as a child's head) that the field was always called by my sons 'the stony field.' . . . I remember doubting whether I should live to see these larger flints covered with vegetable mould and turf. But the smaller stones disappeared before many years had elapsed, as did every one of the larger ones after a time; so that after thirty years (1871) a horse could gallop over the compact turf from one end of the field to the other, and not strike a single stone with his shoes. To anyone who remembered the field in 1842, the transformation was wonderful. This was certainly the work of the worms."

Darwin published his earthworm opus, *The Formation of Vegetable Mould Through the Action of Worms, with Observations on Their Habits*, in 1881. This was late in the evolutionist's life, and his detractors pointed to the work as proof that the old fellow had gone bonkers. Who but a crazy man would spend hour after hour on his knees, handing earthworms leaves and little pieces of folded paper to see which way these beasts would pull his offerings down their holes? (Darwin was trying to determine his earthworms' IQ, and he concluded they had enough brains to pull leaves into their burrows pointy-end-first. Which shows more intelligence than the Long Islanders I've studied who insist on ramming their big fancy cars into supermarket parking lots already impossibly jammed due to the survival-of-the-fittest instinct that takes over during a snowstorm.)

Darwin had a number of volunteers, usually English gentlewomen, observing worms in their own gardens, and one lady noted with interest that earthworms plug up the mouths of their burrows at night. She probably had crocheted as many doilies as humanly possible and so turned to more interesting work. This woman actually took the time to remove every stone from every burrow—to see what would happen next.

"She went out on the following night with a lantern," reported Darwin, "and saw the worms with their tails fixed in their burrows, dragging the stones inwards by the aid of their mouths, no doubt by suction." She told Darwin that "after two nights some of the holes had eight or nine small stones over them; after four nights one had about thirty, and another thirty-four stones." One stone, she reported, which had been dragged over the gravel walk to the worm's burrow, weighed two ounces. Which doesn't sound like a lot, but that's about sixty times the weight of an earthworm, which makes it about as strong as an ox.

Had I such strength, for example, I'd shovel my driveway a lot faster than I'm writing this column. Anyway, Darwin said there were several theories as to why earthworms liked their burrows closed: to keep rain out, to keep predators out, to keep drafts out. Darwin favored the last. Earthworms, he surmised, were civilized enough to seek comfort. Which is more than I can say for some people, who have to dig out their driveways in subzero weather while the dumb old earthworms are snoozing away underground. So much for the big fat brain.

But I wish them a happy winter. And a happy spring, which is their mating time. Every earthworm, by the way, has male and female organs, but they're sociable enough to not fertilize themselves. Rather, they wriggle out of their holes in the evenings, keeping their tails anchored to their burrows, and sort of glue themselves together for a short time. After exchanging sperm, they go their separate ways, later depositing fertilized egg cases beneath the soil surface. One or two baby earthworms hatch out about 30 to 100 days later, depending upon temperature and moisture conditions. Earthworms reportedly live as long as ten years, which is quite a long time if all you do is plow, or eat, or whatever you want to call being an intestine of the earth.

But some days, when I'm shoveling snow, just so I can go to work, just so I can eat, I see that I am not all that far, on the evolutionary scale, from the earthworm. And for an instant, I envy them down there, asleep in their cozy burrows, while I am up here, above ground, freezing my supposedly more highly developed tail off.

Back to Earth

*T*aking a vacation from the garden is a calculated risk. You know the best stuff will ripen while you're away, and if the raccoons don't get it, the neighbors will. Then you worry about who's going to water. And if the weeds and vine borers will take over. And if the lima bean fence will crash to the ground.

But it's worth getting away, because there's always that low point in August, for me anyway, when the suggestion of yet another batch of fresh pesto makes my skin crawl.

So there I was, riding the waves on my boogie board in California and watching the sun plop into the Pacific like a big ripe tomato, not missing the ones back home at all. The closest I got to fresh produce was the hot sauce I ate on my corn chips.

I worried about my garden a little, but I felt fairly safe.

Smug, even. Because I'd bought a fancy new automatic sprinkler before leaving town.

The Gardena water brain had cost me a whopping $79
plus a twenty-minute phone call to company headquarters in
Minnetonka, Minnesota, to figure out how to program the
thing. But the friends who usually pinch-hit for me were going on their own vacations, and besides, I thought, maybe I
should see if these things really work.

Well, there's nothing wrong with the product. Somebody
next door, while apparently watering his plants, had un-
hooked my hose, attached his own and never reattached
mine to its new brain. So, while I was blissfully floating in
trillions of gallons of water, my garden was beached.

No water for ten days, under an August sun, can be a bit
discouraging for a plant, even with mulch up to its knees. But
in the middle of the second week, friends tell me, it rained,
so nature took over where the sprinkler—or the guy who un-
hooked it—had let me down. Still, I wonder if the peppers
are a bit small, and the eggplants stopped producing, and the
tomatoes are still green, from getting parched.

Or from getting choked out by weeds. I may not have mastered the green pepper, but I have a green thumb for crab-
grass, nutsedge, wild buckwheat, sorrel, dock, foxtail,
purslane, chickweed, spurge, mullein and lamb's-quarter.

Fortunately, this last weed is edible, so I knew I'd have
something to eat when I got back home. Lamb's-quarter is
as tasty as spinach, and high in iron, so it's a great salad
green.

But two weeks of chilling out in La-La Land only made
me feel guilty as I looked out over my jungle the first humid
night of my return. A gusty rainstorm had blown down the

lima bean fence to a 45-degree angle and my spider flowers were learning how to survive as hunchbacks. The raccoons, who hop over the garden wall whenever they feel hungry, had crashed through my favorite cactus dahlia, Duet, and the burgundy and white flowers were blooming on the ground.

There was a beer can among the wreckage, which I assumed hadn't been left by the raccoons. Like overfed Romans, they just leave their half-eaten Supersonics lying around for the garden slaves—me—to clean up. But they don't drink beer, not out of cans, anyway.

I mournfully ate a few lima beans from the leaning fence, and decided that the spider flowers could be hunchbacks until tomorrow. Jet lag puts a damper on pounding bean poles with a sledgehammer. So I just picked a few more beans, and a bit of Ragged Jack kale, and a little parsley, and dug up a couple of potatoes, and headed for the house.

My dog and cat were waiting for me, by their empty food dishes, with their own axes to grind. The postcards had never arrived. Nobody had come to play with them. The fleas were having a field day.

Chill out, I said. Read a little P. D. James. Get into boogie-boarding. Eat some chiles rellenos. I started cooking the potatoes and the kale and the lima beans, because there was nothing in my refrigerator but a box of beef-flavored doggy bones and a little carton of cat Yummies.

I like kale, steamed simply in the water it's rinsed with and sprinkled with a few drops of vinegar. Like mustard greens, it has a bite to it without being unpleasantly bitter, and it's packed with vitamin A. I stood over the stove, stuffing green leaves in my mouth, and thought it wasn't so bad to be back, after all.

I told Molly and Mr. Grey how dumb the dogs and cats out there were. "Too much surfing. Sun's fried their brains." They kept their backs to me, but their ears perked up.

Then the potatoes were done. Little buttery yellow Bintjes and pink-skinned Ruby Crescents that I'd coaxed through the beetle blitz and too many hours of unforeseen shade from the garden wall. I just ate them with a little butter and chopped parsley, and savored that flavor of new potatoes, just dug from the earth.

It's an earthy taste, alive with the essence of the ground that's nurtured it. As sweet and nutty as a codfish just lifted from the sea.

After the potato course, I had lima beans, which most people say they can't stand. But that's probably because they suffered six years of the canned variety in elementary school. Or a father who sat over them after everyone else had left the table, saying, "No *Wagon Train* until you eat your lima beans."

But there's something elemental, compelling even, about a garden-grown lima bean. It has a stick-to-your-ribs texture, a satisfying shape—like a little green pillow—and a flavor that needs only a bit of butter, salt and pepper to make me, at least, wish for a fieldful. But these limas, that first night back in the real world, gave me strength. I vowed to pull the fence back up, and do what I could for whatever else was surviving out there in the jungle.

The next day, the air was cool, and the light had that fine clear edge of fall. I started pulling shoulder-high weeds and dousing everything with sea kelp. I tied up the lima bean fence, and deadheaded faded dahlias and zinnias, threw cucumbers the size of rolling pins on the compost pile and found enough eggplants for ratatouille.

Some things didn't seem to miss me at all. The morning glories are a cascade of blue. And at night, the garden drifts in the sweet perfume of my big white moonflowers.

There are some things I'll never be able to change. Like the raccoons. And the fact that I'll never be a neat and tidy gardener. I try to be, but by August, there's always some book, or wave, or friend calling, to take me away from those vital garden activities I forget to remember.

So I'm always amazed when my garden forgives me. This morning, I picked some zinnias, a few spider flowers, dahlias and cosmos, and brought them in a Mason jar to the office. I work under fluorescent lights, in a five-foot-square cubicle like hundreds of others on the same huge floor. I can't see that clear fall light, because the window blinds are closed, to keep the glare off the VDT screens. But the flowers, perky and humorous in their glass jar, hold the sun in their crisp colors.

They don't even know they didn't get watered while I was on my boogie board, out in California.

Game for a Cat

*I*t all started with a field mouse. He'd gotten used to getting his meals in my garden all summer long. And one chilly night, when I brought those last tomatoes indoors, he decided to tag along. In the morning, the biggest, reddest tomato had toothmarks all over it.

"Time for a cat, Molly," I said to the dog who has been my soul mate since my divorce. She just gave me her bored look and nodded off to sleep.

A few days later, I locked eyes with the mouse. I discovered him poaching at the bottom of Molly's fifty-pound bag of Purina Dog Chow.

"Eeeeeeeeeee!" we both shrieked. Then I noticed how cute his big pink-lined ears were. A sort of Dumbo the mouse.

In a fit of compassion, I took the bag outside and turned it on its side. But instead of scampering back to his field, he scurried under the porch—and disappeared through a hole I'd never noticed before. He knew a sucker when he saw one.

He made his next appearance a few evenings later when I was having a heart-to-heart on the phone.

"I don't know," Rosalie was saying. "Maybe my father is right—you can get used to anybody. Love comes later . . . or is my mother right? If you have to wonder if you're in love, you're not . . ."

The mouse came out from behind the refrigerator, crossed the floor to Molly's dog dish, opened his jaws impossibly wide to accommodate a lump of Purina and made his way back to behind the fridge.

"I know what you mean," I said, poking Molly awake, as the mouse returned for a second load. "Maybe I should give that nurseryman another chance. Except his favorite book is *Hortus III.*"

Molly just gazed at the mouse plundering her food supply and went back to sleep. Maybe dogs have a secret pact with mice—based on their mutual aversion to cats.

"Okay, you wimp," I said, as I hung up the phone. "We need a hunter in this family. Somebody who won't faint at the sight of blood."

For years, Molly has failed in this area. When the groundhogs and deer of Ipswich, Massachusetts, began hanging out in our garden like hungry truckers at a diner, I staked Molly to the corn fence.

She spent the night howling.

Her track record hasn't picked up any steam on Long Island. The raccoons ate most of the corn—while Molly lay snoring in front of the evening news. The only live game she ever chases is on the couch—with her eyes closed and her paws frantically pushing her across some dreamscape.

Game for a Cat

So around Labor Day, I returned home with Mr. Grey, a gray kitten, whose white bib and paws and self-assured ways give him the air of some preppie dressed up in his father's tuxedo. Mr. Grey's previous owner had made this cat out to be a great mouser: not even four months old, and he'd hung two dead mice from his belt.

He certainly seemed the feisty type. He marched into my house with no sign of the separation anxiety my *You and Your Cat* book had warned me about. Instead of scuttling off to some safe hiding place to get his bearings, Mr. Grey leaped for Molly's tail, as if this were some fabulous new kitty toy— and then bit me ecstatically in the ankle. (*You and Your Cat* calls this a love-bite.)

"Ow!" I yelled, hitting Mr. Grey on the head (something *You and Your Cat* advises against). Molly gave me a long look that said "See?" and stalked off to her cave in the laundry room.

For weeks, Molly gave me the cold shoulder. When I chatted about my day, she turned her back. If I tried to give her a hug, she left the room. Even rides in the car—her favorite activity—failed to wipe that sullen, depressed expression from her face.

This silent treatment filled me with guilt. I was the betrayer. After all she'd done for me. Who'd offered her furry old coat as a pillow for my bitter tears? Who'd grinned from ear to ear at my stupid jokes? Who'd politely moved off the couch when some new male visitor showed up for dinner?

And all for what? To find herself the punching bag for some ridiculously gregarious animal who was unable to take no for an answer. At night, after the lights were out, I would hear Mr. Grey leaping on Molly and Molly's groans of annoyance. Occasionally, I'd hear her jaws chop the air in a counterattack, but it was always halfhearted. I considered enrolling both of us in an assertiveness-training course.

"I don't like him either, Molly," I admitted one night, about the fortieth time Mr. Grey tried to take a nap on my head. I flung him across the room like a beanbag, another thing *You and Your Cat* frowns upon.

Mr. Grey ran cheerfully back to my chest, where he proceeded to knead me with his sharp little claws and purr joyfully in my face—a noise about as soothing as a Mack truck without a muffler. Then he let out a happy little burp.

"Thank you," I said, reliving the joys of 9-Lives Chicken and Liver Dinner. Which, in case you don't have a cat, has a smell too nauseating to describe in a family newspaper.

I kept telling myself it was worth it. No more mice. I could let guests help set the table for dinner—without fearing they would find those little black offerings in the silverware drawer.

And maybe Mr. Grey would be an asset in the garden. He could lie on the soil in the spring, to warm it up. He could develop a taste for Mexican bean beetles. He could eat deer.

Molly just ignored me. I was a twit. She *liked* mice. They made little caches of her Purina—behind the bookcase, under the couch. And like a kid looking for Easter eggs, Molly liked to find them. Now she had to wolf down her meals in a single gulp—before the purring machine finished his and headed for hers.

Just when the tide began to turn is difficult to say. I began thinking Mr. Grey was sort of cute—especially when he fell asleep with his paw on my arm. I'd find myself petting him when Molly wasn't looking.

But I wasn't the only one. When I wasn't looking, Molly would give Mr. Grey a little playful swipe. Her tail would thump when he ran under the couch. She'd watch for his white paw to reappear—then grab his whole head in her mouth.

Now they play so long and hard, Mr. Grey gets soggy.

The night the three of us watched *Cheers*—my head on Molly's rump, Mr. Grey on my chest—I realized that this cat had weaseled his way into the bosom of our family.

I'm beginning to appreciate cats, like a new vegetable I thought I hated. I like how self-possessed they are. If you don't like them, that's your problem. Besides, you'll change your mind. Until then, they'll just go about enjoying themselves. Molly and I could take lessons from Mr. Grey.

As for the mouse family, it's growing, too. One night I heard scamperings in the kitchen, sounds of things crashing to the floor.

Go to it, Mr. Grey! I thought, picturing my feline hard at work. Then I felt a little furry paw on my arm. Mr. Grey was asleep, dreaming of Nine Lives, no doubt.

I carried him downstairs and introduced him to the enemy. He sniffed the air and assumed what I call his "mouse crouch." I went back to bed with high hopes. But next morning, another tomato had been ravaged, and so had Molly's box of dog treats.

I haven't given up. Organic controls are a slow process. And today Mr. Grey bit the head off his toy mouse. Or was it Molly? They've started sharing each other's toys.

Sometimes It's a
Bad Match

I killed my best friend's African violet. She went off to be an artist in Los Angeles and wanted a good home for the plant she's had longer than her husband.

"I bought this plant twelve years ago at the Stop & Shop," she said, when she first came by with my furry little foster child. "That was three years before I even *met* Steve." She spoke with that tone of voice people use for the old beloved dog they had long before Baby.

We set it in a south window, next to my giant Jade (my only other houseplant). Penny kept turning it this way and that. "Want a comb?" I asked. It was blooming happily, its green leaves as round and flat as pancakes.

I stroked a fuzzy leaf doubtfully.

"Don't do that," Penny said. "They're very delicate."

I put my hand in my pocket. The truth is, I don't like houseplants. I've grown fond of Jade simply because he's survived so many traumas: the time I dropped him on my turntable (he lived, the turntable died), the night my ex-husband read an article on pruning and left him with less foliage than our TV antenna. Jade was part of the family.

But I felt nothing for this African violet. In fact, they are my least favorite plants. My grandmother used to grow them on the gloomy windowsills of her room on the north side of the house. As a kid, I had to help water them (from below), pinch off the dead leaves, count out three drops from the eye dropper as nearsighted Grandma mixed the bloom booster, all in the hopes of getting one of the Reese's peanut butter cups she kept hidden in her highboy. I still can't figure out how those things bloomed at all in that dark room, unless they were some funereal strain.

I tried to pay attention as Penny showed me how the clay pot rested on a saucer of little pebbles, and warned against watering from above. That would spot the leaves, she said.

It liked to stay moist, but too much water would rot the crown. It liked sun, but too much would spot the leaves. (How was I to tell the difference between sun spots and water spots? I felt too inhospitable to ask.) Not enough sun and it would stop blooming—also a symptom of too much sun.

What a confused plant, I thought. But I kept my mouth shut. Penny was already showing the trauma of pulling up her own roots. She'd gone downtown and gotten an L.A. haircut—lawn-mower style. Her husband was talking about "joining" her there. She didn't need me cutting down her African violet. Besides, I wanted to be kind to it—as a way of communing with my soon-to-be-lost friend.

The first month, my visitor did fine, and I decided maybe some of my best friends were African violets. I even considered getting another one to keep it company—one of those fancy varieties with the crinkled blossoms. But then one morning, I noticed a few blooms had dropped off, and there—like some long-feared suspicious-looking mole suddenly appearing—were a few brown spots.

Okay, so I'd watered from above one day when I was feeling impatient. But I'd been careful not to touch the leaves. What a wimp, I thought. A month at summer camp, and you're crying to go to the infirmary.

But I felt guilty. Maybe this plant was picking up on my lukewarm vibes. My real feeling is that plants belong outside. Books, rugs, espresso pots belong inside. Maybe a person or dog or two. Even a cat. But no vines or stupid philodendron creeping over the windows.

I confess I don't feel on solid ground with a potted plant. Outside, I trust my instincts concerning light, temperature, wind and soil conditions. But inside my house, what the Chinese call "dis-ease" sets in, a nagging fear that whatever I do—water, not water, above, below, mist, don't mist, direct light, indirect, repot or not—will be exactly wrong.

It's like being afraid of holding the baby because you'll drop him on his head. And just like the infant who wails when a nervous pair of arms tries to hold him, Penny's African violet was screaming for its mother.

I ran to the local library and took out everything they had on gesneriads. A bulletin from Cornell University informed me that the African violet, or *Saintpaulia ionantha*, is one of "our most popular flowering plants." According to expert Charles Clayton Fischer, "this popularity is justified because the African violet is a handsome plant, easily grown, readily propagated, and the only potted plant to bloom the year-round in the home."

I read that section to my adoptee, who by now had that

flabby bland look of a very old person confined to a hospital bed.

However, Fischer went on, some "unfortunate myths . . .
persist concerning its culture."

For years, he said, the battle had raged over proper watering practices—the below contingent insisting that capillary
absorption was a must; the top types arguing that only watering from above drained harmful salts from the soil.

The truth was, Fischer said in that clear, reassuring tone of
his, the African violet didn't give a hoot which way you watered. What caused the brown spots was the temperature of
the water. Like a little baby, it liked its formula wrist temperature. And it didn't like drops in air temperature either.

"Exposure to 55 degrees will brown the foliage and severely damage the plant, if not kill it," he said. (I edited that
part out of my reading-aloud.)

So that was it. I'd been watering straight from the well. I
also heat with a woodstove, and if I'm gone all day and the
fire goes out, the room temperature drops to 50. When the
stove is fired up, the air leaps to 80 and gets dry as a bone.
No wonder my African violet was foundering. I studied the
pathetic photos of the gesneriads with "cultural problems":
mine looked like them all.

The worst part was, friend Penny called to announce she
was coming east. She arrived at the plant's deathbed.

"What have you done," she said, staring down at the few
brown leaves that had shriveled up around the crown. "You
watered from above, didn't you."

I tried to read her the words of Charles Clayton Fischer,
but she waved me aside. Her punk haircut was even shorter.
She had a sophisticated, foreign look. Avocados, she told
me, grew in her backyard. Had I heard of Wally Ware? she

asked. I tried to lead the subject back to her African violet's demise and my own neglectful behavior, but she would have none of it. The pain was too great. Or perhaps she was simply into other things—and I was left with my guilt, and the empty dish of pebbles.

After Penny left, I dumped the little pot out on my compost and apologized to the remains. I feel terrible when I kill something, even an ant. What if I came back as an African violet?

Now, every time I go to the garden center, I wander by the *Saintpaulia* table. I sort of miss those fuzzy leaves. But I'll wait a while. I don't think I'm cut out for African violets.

The Love of a Dog

Most of my friends have old dogs, by now. Or very young ones, because their old dog died.

The other night, my friend Penny called from L.A.

"We took Sasha to the vet this morning," she said, her voice cracking. "It was awful. He wouldn't even let us stay and hold her head while he gave her the injection."

How horrible, I said, and cursed the man. How lonely for Sasha, to die on a vet table, with no friends by her side. The smart old shepherd used to follow us all around, talking constantly, as she herded us into the living room or kitchen. Shepherds like to keep their herd together.

"Steve and I stayed up last night," Penny said. "We lay on the floor, on either side of her, remembering all the times we had together. Like how she and Molly used to run in the marsh behind your house. And the night she ate the turkey.

She liked having us there, I think. She couldn't get up, but her ears moved. I guess it made us feel better."

Molly was lying on my own bed, which is forbidden. All four legs were stretched out luxuriously, her paws twitching in a dream. Sasha was her favorite dog friend. They were fellow swamp rats. Passionate play-fighters. Jealous dogs in the manger. Molly would want the dog bed only if Sasha was on it. Then she'd chew passionately on Sasha's slimy old ball, just to get her off; then drop the ball and dive for the bed. But Sasha could catch a ham scrap, on the rebound, off Molly's nose.

But all that's in my mind, not Molly's. When Penny called, she didn't even flick an ear. Molly doesn't know the meaning of the verb "to die."

"Sasha's dead," I told her when I hung up. She opened one eye and closed it again. I stroked the soft hairs of her muzzle, not wanting to think about how gray they're getting.

I shed a few tears for Sasha, but some of them were for our mutual past. When Steve and Penny and my husband and I, and our two dogs, all romped on the beach together. When we felt we had our whole lives ahead of us. When we'd sit up half the night drinking Dos Equis, telling funny stories, trusting one another with our dreams.

Molly's a mutt. A Saint Bernard squished into a setter's body, with the personality of the cowardly lion. She was our practice kid, and I got her in the divorce. Her face is half Howdy Doody, half Groucho Marx. Her motto: Fun Forever. She looks great in a wool cap and shades.

She rides in my Trooper with her white ruff puffed out, staring through the windshield, like some nervous aunt. "All clear, here. No, don't go yet. Car on your left!" When she gets bored, she puts her paw on my arm, and I turn on Fine Young Cannibals. I think she likes the beat, because she opens her mouth and lets her tongue hang out. It looks like a grin, to me, unless she's just thirsty. But I swear she grins even more, when I grab her paw, and we boogie in our seats, until the light turns green.

On nice days, she rides with her nose out the window, mapping out Long Island by its pizza, salt air, dry-cleaning chemicals, diesel fumes, Wonder Bread, garbage dumps, fish fries and the like. If I have a Dorito, she gets a Dorito. It just feels so rude, not offering the other person one, too.

I know this dog better than almost anyone. What she likes to eat, and where she likes to wander in the swamp. How rough the pads of her paws are, and which of her old toenails are scarred. I know where she likes her stomach rubbed, and that place inside her ear that sends her into an alpha state. And she knows more about my life, in her doggy way, than anyone I know.

She's the self-appointed guardian of my affections, placing her body between me and some new friend, on the couch. When I tell her to get down, she gives me a black look and lies, with a groan, on the floor, never closing her eyes. When the cat jumps on the bed in the middle of the night, Molly's jaws snap in the dark.

She's my barometer of rocky weather: Let people in the room raise their voices or use a nasty tone, and Molly begins to blink as if someone had just whacked her over the head. Her lips flatten out, making her look more platypus than dog.

It's easy to love a dog, because a dog doesn't talk back. There are no arguments about which movie to see, or where to live, or whose work is more important, or who's in the mood for love. A dog just loves you back, even if you're fat.

I know Molly couldn't invent a spaceship, or a world war, or answer the question of "To be or not to be." Molly has never looked me in the eye and said, with tough love, "I heard you lying to that nice guy who had the theater tickets. You weren't sick. You hung up and ate a whole bag of Cape Cod Potato Chips." She has never curled her lip, when I crawled from desk to bed and pulled the covers over my head, and sneered, "You know, Jane Austen didn't write *Pride and Prejudice* at twenty-one by sleeping all day." Which is, when she holds her tongue, what I could learn from her: that a little more unconditional love might strengthen my human relationships.

I don't think of trading Molly in when she barks once at some stranger at the door and then runs for safety beneath the bed. That's just Molly, I shrug. Somehow it's harder to accept imperfect people.

But at least they live longer than dogs. The painful deal with animals is this: They love us, no questions asked, but we have to go on without them.

Lately, when I notice she's a little gimpy and no longer bounds down the beach like a wound-up clockspring, I push dark thoughts of Molly's death away. I concentrate, instead, on the way her head is turned into the wind, and I try to smell what she is smelling and feel the air that ruffles her coat.

One Life to Live

Sometimes I wish I had a daughter so I could be the kind of mother my mother is to me. I'd like to pass on the treasure she's given me, so freely (I don't say easily) it's almost as if she couldn't help herself. As if we were friends the moment I was born.

Sometimes you feel this way about another person, and that is rare. But if it's your mother, it's as if the cosmos has given you a gift.

Oh, I suppose I'd do a few things differently. Like show my anger more, so that my daughter could see that it's a natural emotion. That it won't kill anyone, or make them go away. (And if they do, you wonder if they loved you, or were just cashing in on the good times.)

I see now, though, how she's right about being careful. Angry words can wound so deeply, the wounds may not heal. And then where does all your honesty get you?

My mother was seventy-seven last week, and I went down to Maryland for her birthday. We walked in the filmy green woods, admiring the dogwood and looking for jack-in-the-pulpits, going a bit more slowly than we used to, but still talking, like girls together, about the important things.

She mentions a man I almost married, who might drop by next time he's down in Washington. Fine, I say. It really isn't. But I can't stop life from making its connections, after I've said no. I saw him just a few months ago, I tell my mother. Just to make sure it wouldn't be worth trying. After all, he likes the country life. He has a good career. Loves kids.

And he travels a lot, my mother said, with a giggle. You could write. He wouldn't be around *all* the time.

Yeah, I say. But something in him makes me want to escape. Then I mention this perfectly ridiculous thing. Something I'd find endearing, if that spark were there. But which, because it isn't, I see stamped on all the "future" kids' faces.

She whooped with laughter. "I know what you mean," she gasped, an old lady, laughing like a girl, right in the middle of the field. I loved her for that. For getting me.

Oh, I have my secrets. And I know now, there are things she'd rather not know. That she wouldn't approve of. But it isn't the report card that either of us is interested in. The world judges you. It takes a friend to want to hear your story, no matter where it goes.

My mother's mother judged her, always. How she looked and how she thought and whom she was with. But at her funeral, my mother wore a beautiful hat that her mother had loved, in her honor.

My mother says she wants us to dance at her funeral, around the funeral pyre. Because she wants to go up in flames, rather than be buried beneath the pink marble tomb-stone my father has already picked out.

It's one of those differences that weighs on you. But if he goes first, she'll probably join him, eventually, under the stone. Because that's how their love has been. I'd like to think that if it's the other way around, he'll agree to the flames, but that would be like snow in August.

I'm shocked at how old she's getting. In my mind's eye, she's still the dark-haired woman who used to sing "Clemen-tine" at the top of her voice, and get us kids to do the same, when we'd start bickering in the back of the station wagon. Who taught us, in her flowered bathing suit, how to go up over the crest of a towering wave, a millisecond before it crashed to the sandy bottom of the Delaware beach. Who told me, at a tender age, all about menstruation, and then plunged into the mysteries of the universe, like why we have the same cycle as the moon.

Ask my mother about the meaning of life, and she's apt to tell you a creation story from Tibet. She reads in the morn-ing, at the kitchen table, before anyone else gets up. And it's as likely to be Will Durant as Anne Tyler. She has her own religion, a combination, I'd guess, of Buddhism and Chris-tianity and Sophocles.

She says it's still a surprise when she looks in the mirror and sees an old lady with wrinkles. You always see yourself, in your mind's eye, as young and vigorous. Because your spirit doesn't age. Or rather, it gets better, with age. When I see twenty-five-year-olds look at me in that "She's too old to understand" way, I want to say, "Oh no, I'm not, it's you who don't understand," but I know it's useless. Maybe you have to get old to like people with lines. The cracks are disappoint-ing at first, but if you keep looking, they get interesting.

I feel as if I carry my mother around with me, laughing at life's ridiculous moments, and grieving over its losses. Or sharing my adventures. Staring into the eyes of a jaguar made of stone, inside a Mayan pyramid in the Yucatán. Leaning into the wind on a dune out in Montauk. Bumming a cigarette at Patsy's Homeport Lounge, my favorite country bar in Bay Shore. But it hurts that she's missing all this, that we live so far apart. I long to lock arms and traipse over to the Bleecker Street Luncheonette for pesto soup, and hunks of fresh, wheaty bread at the counter.

Maybe I'll never have a daughter. But I can be a mother to some of the girls already out there in the universe who could use a second one. And I'm realizing something else. That voice that I carry around with me, that eye, that consciousness I think of as my mother. It isn't my mother. It's me.

Digging Clams
and Other Things

I dug clams with a friend early one morning on a tidal flat somewhere in Smithtown. I'm sworn to secrecy as to just where this spot is, but it's a place where pure spring water runs into the harbor, and watercress grows just behind the high water mark.

We had about an hour of low tide left, before slack tide, that moment of hesitation when the water grows quiet for a few minutes and time seems to stop, ever so briefly, before the water starts flowing in again. Somewhere up there a full moon circled earth, pulling the oceans with it, gathering the water around my green hip boots, as I tried to get to know my clam rake.

"Listen for that squeak, squeak," said Joe, whose bucket, hanging from an old belt around his waist, was a lot fuller than my own. I dragged the rake across the bottom, listening as if my ears were eyes, but every squeak I heard brought up a rock. Or sometimes, nothing. Even a rock can escape a novice's rake, until that flip of the wrist—rather like scooping a ball out of the air with a lacrosse stick, only this is under water—is mastered.

"How can you tell the difference between a clam squeak and a rock squeak?" I asked, digging up another rock.

Joe shrugged. "It's just different."

I like to learn this way. Like learning to float or ride a bicycle. You can't imagine it before you do it, but you have to imagine it in order to do it. And then you never forget.

It was a cool morning, with wisps of clouds riding a slow northerly breeze. Not much happening in the human sense, everything happening in the natural sense. Hundreds of airholes pocked the fine sand at the water's edge, as fiddler crabs ate their breakfast, and cars piled up, as usual, on the Long Island Expressway, a few miles south. But we weren't sitting among them, breathing carbon monoxide, talking on car phones, giving one another the finger, risking murder. We were out here, listening for that squeak of iron against shell, breathing in the rich aromas of plankton and seaweed and decay, all the fishy life so evident at low tide.

The muscles in my forearm ached, pleasurably. A good honest ache that would develop, if I did this regularly, into strength. Not like the aches and pains you get from hitting a keyboard so many times a day you risk tendinitis, pinched nerves, wrist operations.

Out here, if your back starts to ache, it's only natural to straighten up and rest your eyes on snowy egrets, roosting like piles of Kleenex in an old swamp maple on the shore. Or great blue herons, whose gawky takeoffs make them look more like little dinosaurs than birds.

I began to hear the squeak Joe told me about, and I

dropped a clam or two into my bucket with a satisfying clunk. We went closer to shore, as the tide came in, searching with our feet for the softer spots, which the clams prefer. Sometimes you can feel them with your heel, especially the big quahogs, so good in chowder. Clams can live to be 150 years old. A scientist in Florida found that out and stopped eating them, cold. He couldn't bear the thought of devouring something that had been around before his grandmother.

We don't say much, Joe and I. The silence is fuller than most conversation. Which is why this place is so good for the mind.

"When I was teaching, I'd come out here," Joe said. "There's no pressure coming from the outside, so you can look on the inside. And the little things become little again."

He looked westward, across the purplish plumes of the phragmites, as if seeing again the little mining town in Pennsylvania where he was born. "I don't know how I'd ever go back to the hills."

He doesn't have to. Long ago he discovered the secret to Long Island. That tucked in between the malls and tract developments and exhausted roads packed with volatile drivers are these quiet places of clean water and wildlife that haven't read the reports on PCBs and red tide. Heavy rains may occasionally wash pollutants into these waters, but within a few days of clear weather, they're flushed clean.

We filled our buckets as the moon moved invisibly overhead, pulling the water up about my hip boots. A horseshoe crab moved along the bottom, on prehistoric feet.

"Think we got enough?" Joe asked.

"Yeah, sure, this is great," I said, in my happy, ten-year-old voice.

"That's good," said Joe. "Because I wasn't about to show you the really great place."

We made our way up the beach, where scores of fiddler crabs scuttled across our feet, the males holding their enormous right claws aloft. At mating time, the male does a dance with his oversized pincer, to woo his lady crab, whom nature gave only two tiny, same-sized claws. Maybe that's why we like to get dolled up once in a while, put on a sexy dress and splash on the perfume. Because in the wild, the males wear the red feathers, wave the giant claws.

Joe took me around the cove, to look at the swans. "Go on," he told them. "Swim around. Make scenery."

We dug around a bit, just above the water's edge, for steamers. It's quite an art to feel out the oblong soft shell and pull it quickly, before it burrows out of reach, and gently, so as not to crush its fragile shell.

"Who's going to win? You or him?" Joe asked, as my catch squirted me in the face, with its long, annoyed siphon. "That's why they call 'em piss clams."

There are oysters here, too, growing on top of the mussels that cling to the blades of spartina, or nursery grass.

"Well, look at all the things living here," said Joe, who used to teach biology. "Algae and plankton and zooplankton, tiny hatched-out fish. You're looking at the first two stages of the food web. It isn't really a chain, it's a whole tangle of things, and the less it's disturbed, the greater and more complex the web."

I picked a little watercress on the way home and promised myself I'd come back for some salt hay for my garden. We disappeared into the eight-foot-high phragmites and towering yellow jewelweed, our feet sinking into soft mud. The buckets were heavy, but the thought of fresh chowder kept us moving homeward. Past Jerusalem artichokes and wild mushrooms and carpets of trailing arbutus, and along a road lined with such tall poplars, the light fell in shafts and turned the woods into a shadowy cathedral.

I remember that morning whenever I'm stuck in traffic. I think of steaming clams in beer, and frying bacon, and onions, and cutting up tomatoes and potatoes from Joe's garden. Adding some fresh thyme, and bay leaves, a couple dozen peppercorns and fresh Italian parsley. A few shakes of cayenne: "You can't really tell it's there, but it lightens up the mouth," Joe says.

He can't really explain the "lightens-up" sensation. It's like that squeak squeak of rake against clamshell. Or the secret spots of Long Island. We can't tell you where they are. But you'll know them when you're there.

My Invisible Garden

$\mathcal{S}$ometimes my friend gives me a funny look when I talk about my garden. I was late for dinner one night because I'd lost track of the time, and I tried to explain how it is, in the garden, at twilight.

"I was mulching my potatoes . . . and wondering if marsh hay was too salty or if all those minerals from the sea would be good for them. And then I realized that I still have this fear of plants, you know, because I haven't grown potatoes before . . ."

My voice trailed off. The restaurant was noisy, and we were supposed to order quickly, because the kitchen was about to close. I thought of the wind blowing over my potato plants, now cuddled in their hay. Of the bird, with unusual black and orange markings, that had swooped low over the garden wall.

"And guess what? My cleome self-seeded."

"I think I'll have the tortellini," my friend said.

"They look like little hands," I doggedly went on. "That's how I tell them from the weeds."

She smiled, affectionately, but uncomprehendingly. The funny look. The way I nod at new mothers, friends of mine, when they talk about their children. I know they're recounting something passionate, something I even want to experience, but I can't relate to the words.

Other mothers can, just as other gardeners know what happens when you start out mulching potatoes and stop to wind a pole bean around a string or notice a different bird with a strange marking or see, long after you had given up all hope, that the cleome is up.

That evening, for instance, as the light faded, and the tree branches grew black against the pink sky, I knew it was getting on toward dinnertime, but I felt so peaceful sitting like a child in the warm earth. It was dark as I strained my eyes, searching out infinitesimal parsley seedlings among the weeds.

I'd wandered by the parsley patch looking for my watering can, intending to give the potatoes a dose of sea kelp solution before going to dinner. I'd given up on the parsley, a flavorful, single-leafed Italian variety I'd direct-seeded, and figured I'd have to settle for buying some plants at my local nursery. All they sell is the curly-leafed stuff, which doesn't taste half as sweet. But as I went by, I bent over, just for a look, and there, in the twilight I spied a bit of parsley. The baby seedlings are crinkled, like teeny cupcake wrappers.

I was so happy to see them, these little jokes on my lack of faith, that I had to sit right down and pull a few weeds. Give the parsley some air and light in exchange for coming up. And it wasn't easy, because each seedling was about as big as a flea, lost in weeds as thick as a terrier's fur coat. So I slowed down a little, and paid attention to what my fingers had hold of—weed or parsley—and it got a little later, and a little later.

I'd always thought of weeding as such drudgery. And it was, in my father's garden. Work, pure and simple. Because it was his garden, his vision. It had nothing to do with mine.

But now that I have my own garden, I realize that it exists on two planes. It grows on an earthly plane, of course, subject to the vagaries of sun and rain, the ironclad timing of sunrises and sunsets, the visitations of insects, and my own energy and moods.

But it also exists, in a more profound way, in my mind, where it has been growing for many years now. It's a complex vision of many dimensions that has little to do with the earthly garden, where plants get eaten by insects or succumb to disease or my own neglect. This garden changes every time I discover another flower or an heirloom vegetable or see an old climber rose that might want to scramble up my garden wall—even if I don't plant that flower or vegetable or rose for another ten years. It's a garden that I carry with me like a happy secret, as I go about the clamorous world outside the garden gate.

"I think I'll have the clam sauce, white," I said, closing the menu. I smiled at my friend and saw by her face that she'd had a rough day. But what I was really seeing, with my mind's eye, was the cleome. A sea of tall pink and white spidery blossoms, swaying on the evening breeze.

"So how did it go today?" I asked, thinking how, if I got up early, I'd have time to transplant the baby cleome.

It wasn't that I didn't care what my friend was saying; it's just that the garden, especially in summer, comes in and out of the mind like a love affair. The knowledge that something's waiting for me when I get home.

"Of course she's a snob," I agreed. We were gossiping, as usual, about work. "But she is a good writer."

When could I get over to Muttontown for that aged cow manure, I was thinking. Where could I find a Carefree Beauty rose this late in the season? When was that four-inch-wide netting going to come into Hick's Nursery?

"Midweek," the man had said.

"But my limas are up already."

"Awh, a few more days isn't going to make any difference."

I worried about my limas as we ordered more wine. There was a lull in the conversation, and I started talking about my garden again.

"You've got to see these little lettuces growing all around my broccolis. And there's this perennial I don't even know the name of that somebody gave me last year, just a transplant, and now it's this wonderful huge sprawling purple thing . . ."

I stopped. Enough was enough.

It's okay, my friend said. She feels the same way about trying to take the perfect picture. Her photographer's eye has a vision that reaches beyond the realities of rain or technical snags or falling off a wall and missing the shot of a lifetime.

"I like people who are passionate about things," she said.

And when you're passionate about something, you often, mistakenly, try to get the other person to understand. You keep bringing up little details and profound events, thinking that maybe this time the person will get it, will see what you see.

And maybe she's just tried to tell you something, some inner truth, that went right over your head. This separation between people is more common than their connection.

When my friend wanders by my garden on a perfect beach day, she sees the usual state of affairs. The peas are tumbling sloppily over their fence. The parsley still needs weeding. Something has completely eaten the carrots. That gorgeous purple perennial has stopped blooming. And there I am, a mess. Sweaty and dirty, pushing a wheelbarrow back and forth. Working, it looks like.

"That's the cleome?" she says. "It looks like a weed."

I feel disappointed, for an instant, that she can't see what I see. That she doesn't have a window into my Secret Garden. Where all the cleome is in bloom, perfect clusters of pink and white. But maybe that's good, I think, as I go about, sticking these "weeds" into place. Because a garden is like the self. It has so many layers and winding paths, real or imagined, that it can never be known, completely, even by the most intimate of friends.

Cantaloupe Kings

Way back in May, a Yankee up in Sandwich, New Hampshire, claimed he could grow a better Ambrosia muskmelon than anybody down here in climate Zone 6.

(Known to fellow Sandwichians as the Cantaloupe King of Carroll County, John Mayer was coaxing 500 seedlings along for a Memorial Day planting. His secret was transparent plastic—used to warm the rows to 85 degrees by Melon Day. And the King challenged us to a little contest.)

Well, King John, you better go outside and put a blowtorch on those melons. A lone contender has risen out of his patch in Islip Terrace, his chin already dripping with golden juice.

And so are ours, the informal board of judges (a hungry *Newsday* photographer and myself), that is. We had gotten a letter, you see, from a fellow named John Noller shortly after King John sounded his battle cry from Down East, or wherever New Hampshire is (somewhere near the North Pole, judging by the ripeness of the King's melons).

"In reference to your article on Ambrosias," Noller, a lowly commoner, wrote, "I have been growing these melons for the past three years and I can produce as sweet a melon as John Mayer produces with *less work*."

Then, all was quiet on the Southern Front for a few months—until last week, when a call came in from Islip Terrace.

"Hey, when are you people coming out here? I've been eating melons since July 24. Mine are going to be all gone by the time the *King's* are ripe," Noller said. "How are the *King's* doing, anyway?" The contender had to excuse himself from the phone he was laughing so hard.

Then he mentioned a few of *his* secrets: plain old black plastic that warmed his soil up just fine, a fifty-foot-long melon patch that had been part of an old cow pasture, a compost pile as big as a house, and a solution of Epsom salts and borax.

"Gee, we better give the King a call, Mr. Noller," we said respectfully.

The phone rang quite a while up there at the castle. The King was probably out in his melon patch, praying for sun. Or giving his Ambrosias little paddles to keep afloat.

"We've had quite a lot of rain up here," Mayer said, his voice sounding awfully small for a king. "About six or seven inches just last week."

Could you speak up, King? (Had he been crying?) A noble pause. A bit of throat clearing.

The King rallied: "I think they've done pretty well, considering. . . . It would be better if they had more heat, of course . . . and there's a certain amount of disease with all the moisture . . . and the cucumber beetles wreak havoc every year. But I sprayed them all with methoxychlor. . . . I think they'll probably be ready in a week to ten days. Could you get up here around Labor Day?"

Well, look. Let this poor guy call himself the Cantaloupe King if he wants to. He probably has to wear bearskins and put cats in his lap to keep warm these mid-August nights. We're thinking of sending him a little crown with a built-in electric heater.

Meanwhile, we cantaloupe *commoners* should have worn bathing suits to Noller's house—because we needed a good hosing off after our grueling judging session.

"Oh God," the photographer said, crawling toward the hammock for a little recess. (It had been a rough day: he'd been forced to eat two fresh ears of corn at a previous assignment.) His stomach now had a suspicious melonlike shape, and he showed no interest in traveling to New Hampshire out of some cockamamy idea of fairness.

Noller had been a difficult subject to photograph. Earlier, posing in the patch with his melons, the man could not stop grinning from ear to ear. He looked, well, positively gleeful. Undignified. Almost unsuitable for a family newspaper.

"Could you relax your face a little bit, Mr. Noller?" the photographer asked.

"Sure!" Noller said, grinning away. He held two fat golden melons like some father of newborn twins. (And what person in his right mind wouldn't be gloating, having already eaten *fourteen* this summer, and guaranteed at least twenty more. We counted them, ripening right there in the patch. And who knew how many of those blossoms would develop. The very aroma made us almost fall on our faces in a faint.)

Noller picked a couple more—showing us how a perfectly

ripe melon will just "slip" or part from its stem with the greatest of ease. Each one was perfectly shaped and unblemished, firm to the touch, yet slightly compliant, and a golden color beneath the pale "netting." When we pressed our noses closer, the melons smelled sweet, not musky at *all* (in defiance of their name).

"Get out the smelling salts, Janet," Noller said to his wife.

Back in the judge's room, at a picnic table under the trees, Noller sliced through the first sample, and a bit of golden juice ran down the knife. The two halves were a deep orange, firm and juicy, with hardly any rind to speak of. We tried to wait politely while the portions were prepared. We even used forks—though we wanted to bury our faces in the fruit, lick the tablecloth, run out and pillage the patch for more.

"Ah. Yum," and other judge-type remarks were heard from the judge's table. More melons had to be judged—just to make sure the first hadn't been a fluke.

Finally, we came to a unanimous decision. (Our photographer was snoring by now, but we simply raised his hand in a proxy vote.)

Noller's Ambrosias are the best melons we've ever had— *thus far.* If the *King's* Ambrosias can drag enough sunlight through the pines, and enough nourishment out of the rocks up there in New Hampshire, we're always willing to reconvene the board of judges.

But for now, we're content to just swing in our hammocks and talk garden talk.

"Janet," said Noller. "Tell them about those zuke boats you made with the cheese the other night."

Then, with that natural grace known to common folk,

Noller gave us his own secret melon booster recipe: six table-spoons of Epsom salts (a form of magnesium sulfate) and three tablespoons of borax mixed with five gallons of water.

"I wait until the vines start blooming, and then I just go up and down the row giving them a good soaking," said Noller. "Other than that, I haven't done much. I haven't sprayed once this year. Haven't had any need to."

A Yankee couldn't have put it better.

Oh, and another thing. Noller has all these big vats sitting around in his garden—anything to hold water while it warms up in the sun.

"The last thing a tomato or a melon or a pepper needs is to sit in ninety-degree weather and then get a cold shower from the sprinkler," said Noller. "That shocks the poor things—so every evening I give them all a drink from those containers out there."

Until, and this is a pretty big until, those muskmelons are about the size of softballs. Then Noller just cuts off their water supply—to sweeten them up the last couple weeks before harvest.

"Too much water, you see, will dilute the flavor," he said sleepily. "That's why you don't want a downpour at the wrong time." We nodded, thinking bemusedly about the poor cantaloupe King up there in Whoozitswich.

Awh, let him keep his crown. Our competitive edge had dulled. Maybe it was the sun. Or the sugar from the Ambrosias. Or the bees buzzing in the melon patch. Making more cantaloupes for the commoners.

Gandhi Gardening

I t's been an eerie summer for gardeners. An icicle April that turned into a fireball May. Then it got cool again. Then the drought came. Then the rains came. Now it's the Sahara again. What is this, the Book of Job?

I pray only when I think I'm going to die, which crossed my mind during those storms a few weeks back. What a way to go. A dog sitting on your head, as lightning strikes the answering machine. (Don't tell Crazy Eddie's your PhoneMate was struck by lightning. It isn't covered by the warranty.)

I don't go to church anymore, but I've spent the summer trying to be good, like sending birthday cards on time. But did any rain fall on my garden? Not much. Most of it seemed to roll across the harbor and land on a friend's.

"Wasn't that a great shower we had this afternoon?" he'd say. I'd say I didn't get any. "Really? I haven't watered all

summer and you should see my corn." This man believes in God.

To be honest, this hasn't been my Garden of Eden year. The first peas rotted in the cold ground. The second batch did fine, until it got as hot as the fiery furnace and they stopped producing. The lettuce turned bitter and bolted. The Green Comet broccoli was good, but my coveted Romanescos never headed up. The radicchio looked fine, then turned to slime in the humidity. My tomatoes are green tennis balls, and the vine borers have found the squash.

But the potatoes are good, the limas are coming along, and there's a jungle of basil out there. And I have plenty of pole beans—the size of hot dogs—because I've lost interest in picking. The Japanese beetle crop is tops.

It occurs to me, every summer, that some of us use the weather as an excuse. Not that some summers aren't better than others, temperature- and rain-wise, but a few of us get lazy. A drought, and it's too hot to go out there. If you get rain, it's too wet to work. And when the peppers are scraggly, we blame the rain, not the weeds.

But have you ever noticed how the truly faithful continue to reap big fat sweet peppers, no matter what? "My garden's doing beautifully, thanks to all the bunkers I buried here last summer," said Craig Zaffe, a landscaper who's also the caretaker for the Jennings Beach Association in Cold Spring Harbor. "Remember a year ago, last Labor Day, when bluefish drove a quarter million bunkers into the harbor and there wasn't enough oxygen to support them? I spent three days picking them up and burying them here."

Zaffe admitted it smelled pretty strong for a bit, but he became "one" with his bunker. Zaffe's religion is compost.

"I have to clean the beach every weekend, and I dig all that seaweed and mussels right into the garden," he said.

It works. Zaffe's pumpkin patch looks as if it's going to eat Cold Spring Harbor. He stood by a patch of corn that seeded itself. Okay, so it was horse corn, so it didn't taste that sweet.

"But psychologically, it was sweet, because it came up by itself, out of the compost pile," he said.

Note that loving spirit. Even for horse corn. Even for bunkers. I call it "Gandhi gardening."

"I was going to cut down that little weeping cherry, my noble experiment that failed," said Cliff Soergel, over in Huntington's Community Garden. We stared at a young, bare tree that was dead as a doornail. "But then I noticed how the birds use it as a wait station for the birdbath."

Two robins swooped down, as if on cue, and perched in the dead tree, while a third bird took his sweet time dunking himself and fluffing up his feathers in a concrete bath that sits in the middle of Shangri-La, which is what Soergel calls his little paradise.

"I got that cement birdbath for a dollar at a yard sale," he said. "It's good and heavy so it doesn't get knocked over. Everybody goes swimming in there, even the raccoons." I wondered if I'd fit.

The drought-deluge-drought haven't deterred these flowers. You can almost hear them singing gospels, shaking the walls, if there were any, with their lusty A-mens, even when it's so hot your funeral fan wilts.

There's cleome all over the place, and purple cosmos, black-eyed Susans and coreopsis, purple clematis scrambling up the rose arbor, which is laden with table grapes. Butterflies on the butterfly bush.

"Two weeks ago, I watched a big monarch circling around

here. He made three sweeps and settled right on that bud-
dleia," said Soergel. We sat down in Shangri-La's living
room, which is three rickety metal chairs around an old up-
turned whiskey barrel.

"The top caved in last summer, so I filled it with sand and
put the top back on. Nothing can blow it away now. And nobody's gonna steal it," he said. See, there's nothing negative
about this guy.

"Don't say hot, say warm, it's a more positive word," said
Soergel.

Paul Sattely came by to fill up the third chair. Soergel is
the flower man, Sattely is vegetables. These two meet at
Shangri-La, in all seasons, sipping coffee, watching the geese,
or the catbirds, or the storms roll overhead.

"Yeah, I got about a bushel of Idahos and Irish cob-
blers," said Sattely. He was in farmer's garb, old plaid shirt,
straw hat, dusty boots. Soergel has more of a Crocodile Dun-
dee look.

"I've been harvesting all summer like crazy," said Sattely.
"I had good peas, only the birds got to them before I did."
He didn't say that like he minded. He said it like St. Francis
of Assisi.

The Japanese beetles have been terrible, he said. But he
just picks them off, every morning, and his reward is an
earthly one. There's nothing like a fresh green soybean.

"I say they taste somewhere between a pea and a lima,"
said Sattely.

I headed home to weed, but stopped to visit Bill and Cathy
Barash, two dueling trowels in Cold Spring Harbor. I'm not
sure what their religion is. Food, maybe.

"Cathy's been stealing my gladiolus again. She stuffs them
with tuna fish," grumbled Bill, leading the way to his garden.

"As she says, our successful marriage is based on separate gardens."

The nicotiana needed staking, because it had been bashed by the latest rain I didn't get, but otherwise, the *fleurs* were booming. Compost, TLC, water. That's about all, said Bill.

Cathy was standing in her jungle of tomatoes, mostly green, looking for her watermelon plant. She's an intensive gardener. I felt better when she started complaining.

"You should have seen the sunflower that popped up in the garden from my bird feeder," she said. "It had about twelve flowers on it and I was going to dry the seeds, when we got that deluge [what deluge?] and the whole thing just rotted."

And another thing. "I was very nice with all those swallow-tail caterpillars. I let them demolish my parsley, my celery, my dill. And do you think I've seen a swallowtail in my garden? No. I have none." They're all over at Shangri-La, I guess.

I wanted to ask Cathy if she'd go to church with me this Sunday, but that seemed a little drastic. Maybe I'd better start out slow, and do some weeding.

Climbing Ladders

Sometimes the little things are the great victories. Like getting the storm windows off before the summer solstice. Mine had been on for so long they'd become a metaphor. They're heavy wooden old things, with glass panes that are held on by some mystical combination of crumbling putty and faith. Some have no putty left at all; yet last winter, they hung in there, through the winds that howled across the frozen marsh, and the gusty rains of spring, and the sudden heat of May, when my upstairs got hot enough to hatch eggs.

If you live with a man, he's likely to volunteer for this job. I know we liberated types are supposed to leap around on roofs and fix cars and so on, but I think it takes a while to reprogram our DNA. Maybe our granddaughters will wake up thinking, "Today I'm going to seduce George by putting up all the screens, instead of baking a rhubarb pie," but meanwhile, despite my belief in equality, I am plagued by fear and loathing of ladders and falling, and weak upper arms that can't do even one chin-up, which' is a problem when you're standing on a rickety ladder, trying to lift off a heavy old storm window with one hand because you're afraid to let go of the rainspout with the other.

Actually, a friend of mine put the storm windows on last fall, when he sensed my dual reluctance—that I could neither bring myself to put them up nor ask for his help. I was grateful when he offered, and aware of how easy it looked, when he scrambled up the ladder and ambled about the roof, but I didn't rush to test my feminist principles this spring. I stood in the barn, every weekend, staring at the old ladder. Picturing myself, and it, toppling to the ground. But I never mentioned this to my friend, because, well, we're just friends.

It's different when you live with someone, or you're married. It's part of the cozy intimacy to admit to little fears and the things that you know you should learn to do but never will, unless forced to. Sure, you don't want some Tarzan who always insists on driving, but it's kind of nice to see his eyes roll back on that first bite of pie. Ahh, he says, rhubarb juice on his chin. Ahh, you say, standing in the breeze of the screen windows. But why waste copy on domestic bliss? When here I was living alone, in a house hotter than a chicken coop in July.

I have no problem with the downstairs windows. Standing on a chair does not trigger my fear of heights. And I'd managed to get a few storm windows off upstairs, by unhooking them from the inside, lifting them off their hinges and pulling them in at an angle. All the while thinking, If I had a man around, I wouldn't be doing this. But none of the screens could be put on this way because they all hook from the outside. I could live with a few moths, but when the mosquitoes started to whine and the june bugs to dive-bomb my pillow, I knew I couldn't wait any longer for my prince (or even a frog) to show up on a ladder.

"I have a little job I need some help with tomorrow," I said one Sunday evening, when my best friend and I were lounging on the couch. We'd been drinking wine late, discussing our not-quite-blissful lives and if anything practical could be done about them (What about that guy at the strawberry festival?), when a june bug hurtled into the room.

"I've got to get the screens on," I shouted, as I banged the bug to death with my shoe. (June bugs, if you don't know them, are the size of bumblebees, and they sound like chain saws.) "Only I'm nervous about using the ladder, so I need you to hold it for me."

"Sure. My father taught me all about ladders," she said, perking up. We'd had a little talk about friendship, see. How I'm afraid to ask for help, and then I complain that nobody's helping. I don't trust people, she said. Well, hell, that's scarier than a ladder.

My friend stayed over on my Castro Convertible, reading till the wee hours. I got up at dawn, to dig in the garden, and then, a little later, brought espresso to my nightbird in bed. I went out again, to plant some window boxes. And to my amazement, she appeared on the porch, blue jeans on, under her nightgown, smoking a cigarette and ready for action.

"You're going to kill yourself, for sure, if you leave the ladder that way," she said, casting a practiced eye on where I'd placed it. We set it lower, just beneath the window, and she gave it a hefty shake.

"You're sure it won't keel over," I said, placing a tentative foot on the first rung.

"There's no way this ladder will fall, I guarantee it," she said, in her firm but motherly voice. "I'm right here."

With every step, I pictured the thin rungs snapping like toothpicks, and halfway up, I reached a tentative hand toward the first hinge holding the storm window in place.

"You'll never reach it from there," she said. "You'll have to go farther up. I'm right here. You won't fall. You're doing fine."

Her words were like hands holding up a person who doesn't believe she can float. Only there I was, teetering on air. "You're almost there. One more rung. Take your time."

I felt so awkward, trying to figure out where to place my weight. Leaning my whole body against the ladder, so I could free both hands to lift the heaviest windows. Letting out little "Uh-ohs!" and shameless "Aaaaaahs!" and letting my friend let it be okay.

In slow motion, I'd hand each window down to her up-stretched hands, and she'd hand me a screen back up. Slowly, slowly, moving the ladder about the house, we got all the windows off and the screens on. And suddenly, inside, the summer breeze came in, without the bugs. I gave my friend a big hug. Funny how a little thing like a ladder can stand in your way, if you're afraid to ask for help.

If Geese Could Drive

A few Sundays ago, after a week in the mountains, I returned to Long Island on the Cross Sound Ferry. It was a beautiful evening, with a crescent moon hanging in a purple sky, and the air crisp and salty, as my friend and I left Orient Point and drove through East Marion. When we slowed down, the woman behind us raised her hands from the wheel in exasperation, as if we'd just snatched the very last cart from her hands at the door of Finast. My friend stuck a hand out the window and pointed to the 25 mph sign. The woman gave us the finger.

This gesture, so common to Long Island, was in such contrast to the evening, and our week in Vermont—where people actually slow down to let you in, rather than speeding up to kill you—that it threw me into despair.

"Why did she do that?" I raged. "It's Sunday evening. Where could she be going that thirty seconds out of her life would make such a difference?" All this free-floating anxiety, just waiting to blossom into hate, was suddenly shocking to me. Because I'd been away from it for a while. But you get numb again, quickly, because you have to, to survive the violence.

I turned around and looked at the woman. Her face wore an expression of hatred. She'd been enraged by having to slow down; now she hated us because we'd forced her to acknowledge the low-speed zone.

The next week, I had my usual brushes with death on the highways. Like being in the left-hand lane of the Triborough Bridge when you need to be in the right-hand lane for the Eastern Long Island exit. There was enough room to cross over, until the man in the middle lane decided it would be fun to speed up and kill me. I swerved back into my own lane as he roared by. His friends were laughing in the back and giving me the finger.

My hands were shaking, as if someone had just stuck a gun in my face, only this man's weapon was his car. I think of him as the intentional murderer. But there's another kind who's more impersonal, who doesn't even bother to look back.

This man was zooming down the right-hand lane of the Southern State, in his white Camaro, when he realized, a bit late, that he was in an Exit Only lane. He veered, without looking, into the middle lane, forcing me to veer left, almost causing a three-car accident behind me.

Long after my adrenaline stopped pumping, my mind kept working on this guy. He hadn't even turned his head; he hadn't even acknowledged that he had almost killed me, and others, when "change lanes" registered in his narcissistic brain.

A toddler will do this when his baby sister grabs his toy or wanders innocently into his line of action. You have to watch him, because the toddler may try to kill the baby with an ashtray, because he doesn't have a sense of morality at that age. He isn't civilized. Everything is one big Me. But this guy wasn't driving an ashtray.

I think these people are like warning signals. Like the fish we're not supposed to eat anymore because of all the PCBs and mercury. Or the rabid squirrels that run out of the woods and bite people because there aren't enough trees and acorns to go around.

That woman in East Marion is all of us, driving down a lovely country road. Lights going on in the Victorian houses, kids riding their bikes home for dinner. But did she see any of this, one second of the life going by, never to be repeated, in just that way, ever again? No. Her hands were locked on the wheel, her eyes riveted to our bumper, her mind frozen on whatever—her boyfriend, her job the next morning, the Lean Cuisine in her oven. All else were just obstacles, blocking her straight shot from point A to point B.

She was on a country road, but she was driving as if she were on the LIE, or the Southern State, or the Northern State, or the BQE: roads that numb the mind, as we drive as fast as we can, in one direction, on a three-lane strip of asphalt that renders any landscape—of the natural world, that is—meaningless.

No matter that the road once cut through horse farms and potato fields and beloved old houses. It's all just homogenized bushes and grass to us now. Signs like Deer Park Road and Riverhead have lost their original meaning, because the deer and the rivers are out of sight and out of mind. And because no visible community or inviting side roads lead us away from this one long track of asphalt and cement, there seem only two directions to go in—and no exit. Physically or psychologically.

Look at how we're traveling—one driver to a car, radios blaring, making deals on car phones—barreling through space in an enclosed box full of isolation that renders not only the landscape but also other people meaningless, or obstacles, or both.

One day last spring, I was driving east, past Old Westbury, on the LIE. There was a rare stretch of space in front of me, and to my disbelief, a mother goose and her goslings came out from the bushes and started waddling across the highway—toward our hurtling death traps. It's interesting to me now, how we all tried desperately to avoid the geese—tires screeching, cars wildly swerving—as something primitive in us connected to the birds.

Miraculously, they reached the median strip, but at the wall of concrete, the mother instinctively took flight—leaving her babies scuttling about until, I assume, they died. I didn't see this. Because I had to drive on, as all the others did, to avoid death myself.

I forgot about it, in my numb way, as soon as I got to the office. But like the woman in East Marion, the geese come back to me, now and then. Because we're all being eroded by the same act of hurtling, in our boxes of steel and gasoline, backward and forward along the same straight, look-alike roads. And I wonder, if the geese had been encased in cars, if we'd have even slowed down to let them cross.

Our Aging Farm

*T*he roses have started blooming again now that the nights are cool. Every evening, if he's able, Dad goes out to cut some for the house. Just a little walk around the yard now makes him short of breath, but he says it keeps him alive.

He clips each one and hands it to me to hold. I've come down to Maryland for a fall visit, and the weekend has those brilliant colors of a season coming to its end. Pink, yellow, coral and red. Hybrid teas and grandifloras, varieties my parents bought on a whim outside Woolworth's, or ordered from Jackson & Perkins, or were simply given on some special day. Maybe a hundred bushes, I'd guess, if you count the pale pink polyanthas brought by my grandmother from her father's rose garden, almost a century ago.

"This one's called Patrician," says Dad. "Your sister gave it to me one Father's Day." The deep red, velvety rose smells like a rose should. When my hands are full, we head for the

kitchen, walking slowly, to stick them in a pitcher of hot water and set them in the cool, dark cellar for a few hours.
They last longer that way.

The house is full of them, on the kitchen and dining room
tables, on the piano in the living room, in the bedrooms upstairs, and like the old clocks, which seem to tick louder at
night, the roses are more fragrant in the evening. Or perhaps
I just notice them, as I hear the clocks, when it's quiet.
There's a clock in almost every room, but half of them don't
work anymore, and they sit silently on mantels and antiques
that Mother and Dad keep trying to give away to us kids.

But we don't have room for big old sideboards and mahog-
any dressers. You need a big farmhouse for stuff like that. A
farmhouse like this one, begging for some young people to
move in, fix the clocks, knock down some walls, turn the old
back porch into a sunroom, put a woodstove in the kitchen.

"I've always thought it would make a great bed-and-
breakfast place, or the main building of an artist's colony,"
Mother says, hopefully.

"Yeah, or maybe a school," I say. "Or somebody with
enough money could make a great house out of the barn.
Can't you see the old stone barnyard as an outdoor room,
with climbing roses and clematis?"

My mother and I play this game, though it's a dangerous
one, because it's based on "someday."

As in someday I'll move down there and build a solar
house on the hill overlooking the stream. As in someday I'll
be a novelist, so it won't matter where I write. As in someday
I'll start a nursery down there, full of herbs and perennials
and organic vegetables.

"Sure, look at all those suburban homes around here now.
They're dying for that kind of thing," Mother says. I hate

these suburban homes. They've eaten up the old graceful farmhouses and the rolling fields, and put up houses with fake colonial pillars and little green lawns. But still, they'd buy our plants and our vegetables.

"Yeah, maybe we could even charge admission to see a chicken lay an egg," I say. But even as I say the words, I feel the old farm closing in on me. Or is that claustrophobia merely a failure of courage—to make the vision real.

Mother brightens when we talk like this, but Dad gets depressed.

"None of you kids will move down here. You're all involved in your own lives, which is as it should be. Mother and I might as well sell and move into Fairhaven."

Fairhaven is one of those tasteful "retirement" homes, where people go to wait until they die. It costs a king's ransom to buy into the place, and a few thousand every month just to live there, if you call it living.

"Dad, you could hire a cook and maid and a driver for all that money," I say.

We change the subject, quickly. This farm has always been run by family, but now the children have moved away. Father and Mother are the last king and queen waiting to pass on the scepter.

My great-grandfather built this house a hundred years ago, out of white oak cut from his woods. He built the wide front porch from quartz stone dragged from his fields. His son planted the grapes, and made the grape arbor out of black locust and angle irons salvaged from a windmill that blew down in a hurricane in 1915. The two barns are also of white oak, and my parents have kept them painted and the roofs repaired, just in case one of us should, by some turn of mind, move back home.

But the trees don't believe it. The maples that my grand-parents planted shortly after their wedding day are toppling, one by one. The mimosa tree that used to summon hum-mingbirds outside my bedroom window died a few years ago. The willow that Linda Bond and I climbed for our secret club meetings is just a stump. The pear tree, once laden with sweet, grainy Keefers, has been barren for years now, its trunk as hollow as a flute. Dad plants new trees when he can, but the place needs a stronger back, and the years to see those trees grow tall.

Last summer, a big limb blew off the apple tree, a sweet tangy variety Granddaddy called "Strawberry" because of the seedlike flecks in its bright red skin. He'd planted it in front of the chicken house, which fell down in a storm a decade ago, leaving its stone foundation as bare as an an-cient ruin.

"I meant to take some cuttings from that tree and graft them onto a couple standards," I say to Dad.

"Yeah, I thought you were going to do that," he replies. "But it's too late, now, with that limb gone."

I've put a lot of ideas off. Like the double-file viburnum I was going to plant. A whole stand of them bordering the trees by the stream, so that their white flowers, marching double file down the graceful limbs, would light up the woods in late May. I'd like to plant a wildflower garden in the old chicken yard and try my hand at organic fruit trees. My brother, who has a farm three hours west of here, wants to grow organic corn, to feed the cattle he raises for organic beef.

"That's crazy," says Dad. "He'd lose all his profits just transporting the crop over the mountains."

But he'd love us to prove him wrong.

An orchard takes a lot of care. Somebody living there, to cultivate and fertilize and spray, prune and train the limbs. When you put up a greenhouse, you have to stick around in case the heat fails, or the vents don't open.

It's not like handing the old folks a few tomato plants and flower seedlings, annuals that only grow one year.

"Boy, Dad, those spider flowers I brought down are giants," I say, admiring the seven-foot purple flowers. "They reseed like crazy, you know." I didn't bring them any trees.

"Yeah, I'll have to move them next summer," he says. "They're shading the crape myrtle your mother and I put in this spring. It's a new hybrid that's supposed to be hardy in this zone, so I'm going to mulch it well this fall and see what happens."

It was hard on them, dragging the hose around the yard to keep the plants alive, during the drought. But it kept them going. And even if Dad doesn't believe any of us will see that crape myrtle grow old, it's an act of faith to plant it.

Generations of Gold

This big old house is full of good junk.

Down in the shadowy regions of the cellar are Mason jars and jelly glasses, milk pails and stone crocks laced with cobwebs, clay pots and old nail kegs, tin boilers that once simmered smoked hams for hours on the stove.

The back porch (though it isn't a porch at all but a long drafty room off the kitchen, enclosed by windows that rattle when the north wind blows) is crammed with tables full of pots and pans and cookie tins and meat grinders and badminton nets and croquet sets and a hedge trimmer with about a zillion feet of electric cord. There is an old refrigerator that fills up with beer when the whole clan is here, and a tall old pine cupboard with so much stuff you have to be careful when you open the glass-paned door.

Every closet in every bedroom has that smell of old books (I'm sorry to keep using this word, but this place is *old*), the cheap kind people used to get in sets (the Hardy Boys, Tarzan, Nancy Drew, Zane Grey), only the best one, like *Nancy Drew: The Hidden Staircase*, is always missing. There are boxes of scholarly papers ("The Extinction of the Dinosaurs") and love letters from college ("My love for you is like a big red barn") and suits with impossibly narrow waists and strapless prom dresses, the kind with the puffy crinoline skirts, which are likely to spring out into the room looking for a dance.

Then there's the attic on the third floor.

Mom tries to attack this region once in a great while, cutting trails through the chairs and headboards and box springs and trunks and photo albums (we decided to keep all the pictures of everybody's first wife or husband) and old stuffed animals losing their stuffing.

"Next time you come down here," she says on the phone, "I want each of you children to sort through your things."

There's a radical, energetic tone to her voice. Everything else will go to Goodwill. Or maybe we'll have a yard sale. "People make hundreds of dollars that way," she says.

Yeah, and they just have a few dishes and lamps to sell. We could make millions.

But let her try to throw out one of those chairs missing a leg: "Wait! Wait! We could fix that!"

It's in the genes of farm children to save everything. Who knows when you'll need a piece of wire to get the tractor going? Or some soft twine to help keep the peas up, when they get so heavy the vines start sagging?

This is a gardener's gold mine.

Already I have a collection of assorted crocks that will look fine with blue lobelia trailing over the sides. Or maybe some white daisies with that pale green *Helichrysum petiolatum* tumbling down. And a whole collection of mints to pick for sun-brewed teas poured over ice. Gazania, that yellow flower with the silver leaves, looks great with herbs like marjoram and feverfew.

I've been poring over those coffee-table garden books for weeks now. I figure the old ham boiler is just as good as an eighteenth-century lead trough I saw planted with petunias, scented geraniums, purple sage and marguerites. And when I found the old wooden cart in the barn, I wondered how it would look full of fuchsias.

Whoa.

I've been in the city too long. This is a Maryland farm I've come back to, not some new place in the country trying to look old. The ham boiler should boil ham. The cart should haul leaves.

In the old chicken house, now piled with lawn chairs and ladders and Dad's old barbecue, I found enough seed-starting pots to start a garden supply company. And the leaky wash-tub that Grandmother, who was born in 1880, used for her potting soil.

She died twenty years ago. But I can still see her crouched beneath the pear tree, mixing clay soil with compost and peat, turning it over and over with her trowel until it was as moist and crumbly as chocolate cake. "There," she would say, banging her trowel against the metal tub. "Stick your hand in there. That's how soil should feel."

"Uh-huh," I'd say from deep in the hammock under the grape arbor, where Tarzan talked to the elephants.

In those days, gardening was something to avoid. It was what old people did, unless they had some hot sticky chore like weeding the carrots or picking beans. Then it was what you did for your allowance.

It was only when I moved away that I had the need to plant things. My first garden, fifteen years ago, was a handkerchief of spinach and snap peas, a few tomato plants, some Italian parsley and basil. And three Mammoth sunflowers that grew ten feet tall.

Tending those three flowers was like bringing a shell back from the beach to help me remember the boom and hiss of the waves. In my little apartment, I would look out at their bright yellow faces and think of the sea of sunflowers that once grew in our meadow, turning their heads from east to west as the sun moved across the sky.

As I come home to the farm these long weekends and look out over the fields, I am overwhelmed by the expanse of this easy, rolling land. I remember that I could plant a whole field of something and carry the harvest back in my wooden cart.

Virgil in the
Chicken Yard

I am designing a medieval kitchen garden in the shape of a giant egg. An egg in a square. It's taking shape slowly in the abandoned chicken yard of our Maryland farm.

I've been reading about the great gardens of the world, and a central axis, like the four poles, is etched in my brain. But I can't get my mind to think in linear patterns. It likes circles. So now I have a design that's kind of like a Greek Easter egg. An egg with a cross in it.

It came to me in the reading room of the New York Public Library. I was reading Rosemary Verey's *Classic Garden Design*. The elaborate formal gardens of Versailles, Mrs. Verey writes, were really about dominance and power. The main axis stretched out from the house to the farthest distance beyond. Like the king looking outward over his conquered land.

I looked up at the great rounded windows of the cavernous

room—big enough for ten kitchen gardens—and let my mind dwell on those ancient shapes. The round windows were set into great rectangles of stone, their panes divided into a gridwork of satisfying squares, which let in the soft gray light of spring.

I leafed through the book and stared at my favorite picture: a section of Mrs. Verey's own kitchen garden in England, where fat, round purple cabbages alternated with the more ornate ruffled leaves of green-and-white ornamental cabbages. (Which never made sense to me. A cabbage you can't eat.)

In the very center of the patch sat a rounded copper bowl spilling over with deeply lobed blue-green leaves. Where had I seen that plant before? Was it the bold leaves of lupine before it bloomed? Or a kind of lady's-mantle? That *Alchemilla x splendens* I had longed for from the White Flower Farm catalog? No, those leaves had been a deeper green, with silvery edges and undersides. And they liked partial shade.

What I needed in my bowl was a sun-lover. Like trailing nasturtiums. Or maybe sage, which covers itself with little purple flowers by midsummer. And instead of cabbage, what about tangy mustard greens, alternating with red chard, to get that pleasurable contrast of color? In a kitchen garden, I figure, beauty should taste good.

I stared at Mrs. Verey's cabbages. To my surprise, they were in a square bed, set off by a wide stone-and-brick path that the gardener had built herself, echoing the colorful patterns she had seen in the sixteenth-century vegetable gardens at the Château de Villandry. "One glance," she writes, "should be enough to set several ideas burning in your head." I must go there someday.

Virgil in the Chicken Yard

I looked back up at the windows and felt again that satisfying juxtaposition of circles and squares. As if some geometry as ancient as the round nucleus of a square plant's cell had spun itself into our imaginations and our architecture, our quilts and gardens.

Our farm is a humble empire. It has no parterres, nor vast reflecting pools, nor even a king. The house, elegant in its simplicity, is surrounded by rambling spaces that once had a function, like raising chickens or playing croquet or just hanging out the wash, so people could fall asleep between sheets that smelled of air and leaves.

The paths, so important to a garden, always led somewhere, but in that rambling way that feet travel when taking the most natural route from here to there: from back door to grape arbor, to clothesline, to compost pile, to the shortcut between the mock orange bushes that perfume the kitchen in May.

In the great reading room, I sifted through ideas as old as Virgil and Pliny, who could still imagine the gods coming down to plant. I stared at pictures of the gardens of Pompeii, frozen in time by the lava of a volcano. I tried to digest the vastness of time stretching from those gardens to this room full of people of all ages and colors and obsessions. We read together in silence. Like farmers sitting on the front porch, not having to talk at all.

"A what kind of garden?" Cousin Janice had asked last fall, dropping by with one of her unbelievably sweet melons. She watched me dig up a bed that looked suspiciously round.

Gardeners here plant in straight rows. Even gladioluses. It's the centuries of corn in their veins.

This bed was for my garlic—Long Island garlic grown by friends. And giant alliums and Siberian irises. I had a feeling they would complement one another.

"It's a medieval garden," I said, pounding my spade against clay as hard as rock. "Full of herbs and greens and fragrant flowers. Where everything grows together in geometric patterns."

"You know," she said. "You've got a rototiller over there in the garage. Standing idle."

"It doesn't go deep enough," I said. "Besides, I'm experimenting with half the beds. Not digging at all."

Just layers of newspaper and three inches of aged manure right on top of the wild mown grass of the yard. Let it just turn to compost, the theory goes, without destroying the soil structure below. It's the very opposite of double-digging, which I am trying here as well.

"We'll see which one works better," I said.

"New York gardening," Janice said, and carried her melon off to the kitchen.

Spring is pressing on the windows of the library. It's time to fold up the books and start breaking ground.

I can't wait until the earth thaws and the shoots of garlic poke through the ground. And the first good day when the soil isn't too wet to work and the door of the back porch bangs as I run from house to garden, carrying some forgotten tool or packet of seeds. Retracing the footsteps of my ancestors, but thinking constantly, how can I shift the paths and make them mine?

The Hairy Vetch
Knows

You know how thunderstorms start? A hot air mass bumps up against a cooler one. Like a big fat fantasy hitting reality.

"Hi, Mom. I'm sorry I didn't get down this weekend," I said on the phone last Sunday night.

There was an infinitesimal pause on the other end.

"That's all right, dear," said my mother. But then, she's a Southern lady.

"I should have called . . . ," I said, getting ready to explain how I got tied up at the Philadelphia Flower Show.

(Where I did dally, but then I drove back to the city because I wanted to see a city friend, who doesn't quite get my fascination with carrots.)

"Don't worry," she said. "But I've been awaiting my instructions. The broccoli seedlings are four inches high."

What? I didn't think those old seeds would even come up.

You know how it is. Every spring, you go on a binge, ordering all your favorite seeds: spider flowers, cornflowers, fragrant sweet peas and moonflowers, sunflowers, climbing nasturtiums, Brussels sprouts, basil (can't have enough basil), arugula, Japanese eggplant, jalapeño peppers, and don't forget the leeks.

Then you look in the old roasting pan (don't tell me you store them in film canisters in the refrigerator), and there they all are. Sealed packs of the same varieties. From last year and the year before that.

The experts are always preaching, "Test the viability of last year's seeds by rolling up a few of them in a damp paper towel."

(Anybody who's actually done this, raise your hand.)

If they germinate, you're in business. If they don't, you get to go on another seed-ordering binge.

But this year, I decided to carry out my own germination tests. I tossed them all on seed flats, labeled the rows, stuck them in plastic bags and set them on Grandmother's old marble sideboard.

"All you have to do is spritz them with this if they dry out," I said, handing my mother a plastic water bottle late Sunday night.

I had to get up at five the next morning to get to New York in time to write the column I was supposed to write at the farm, only I didn't get to it because I talked to a man about an irrigation pond, and then I had to take a nap because the fresh air made me so sleepy.

"Don't worry," Mom said. "Bernie has gone into town to find a part that's missing from your grow lights."

(Bernie is the man who keeps things running while all us grown kids are gone, which is most of the time.)

I'd meant to get my old fluorescent lights out of the abandoned chicken house, where I'd stacked them after my last move, but something else always got in the way.

Like life: Having a drink with our old friend Betty, who lives just up the road. Talking on the phone to the man who likes to watch corn grow at the Museum of Natural History. Trying to read *DOS for Dummies* so I can get my computer to work down here in paradise.

And then there are all the other garden projects demanding attention: I ran out to take the mulch off the tulip bed I'd planted along the barn bank. I dug up the pots of bulbs I'd buried and then forgotten about. I talked to the soil conservation man (after my brother Jim and I got to wondering if we'd qualify for an irrigation pond).

"Maybe we better just get the kitchen garden going this year," my mother said as Jim and I warmed up to the pond idea.

"Maybe I could graze my cattle down here," said Jim, a doctor who keeps a herd on the side.

"Yeah, and if we had water, I could grow herbs and perennials to sell," I said.

Mom looked up at the ceiling, as if our wild fantasies were about to carry the roof off the house. Or was she praying?

She was the one who saved the Asian pear trees I planted last spring, before I went back to the city and the drought arrived. Every evening, she carried water to them, out to the barn and back.

She and Bernie were the ones who battled the Japanese beetles and used baking soda instead of Benlate, after I suggested, the summer after my father's death, that we try to grow his beloved roses organically. I encouraged them, on the phone.

As the Maryland earth warms up, and my fantasies take shape, I see that this is no little weekend garden I've set in motion here.

Like the test plots of tomatoes growing in their cover crop of hairy vetch: I haven't even had time to find hairy vetch seed. And here it is mid-March already, when the vetch should be getting hairy.

"Why don't I have Bernie prune that chaste tree?" Mother suggested two weeks ago. It has the most delicate, fragrant blue flowers in late summer, but you have to cut it to the ground every spring.

"No, no, I want to do it," I said, as if tending every plant would make it mine.

But every day, it gets warmer, and the buds are greening up, the sap is running. I need to prune.

Mom says nothing. But I hear a little thunder.

Soon it will be time to plant the peas, and I haven't even spread aged manure over the garden. We could be eating corn salad by now—if I'd planted it. If I weren't sitting here typing in an office near Times Square. If I weren't heading to see *High Heels* with a friend. If I could sit in the old farmhouse at night, without missing the clamor of the city.

It will be a rumbly kind of summer, I think. With flashes of light, way off on the horizon.

I don't know if I cotton to weekend gardening. Growing plants without being there is like having a baby and letting somebody else take care of it.

Never Say Thank You
for a Plant

"Never say thank you for a plant; it won't grow," Aunt Hazel said, biting into a chocolate chip cookie. Actually, she's not supposed to have sugar, but when you're eighty-five, can't you have what you want?

"That's right," Cousin Janice said, passing a plate of homemade sweet pickles. "Grandmother Alban, who lived to be ninety-six, would take a cutting from you and ask how to grow it, but she'd never say thank you. And if you thanked her, she'd take the plant back. Then she'd sneak it into the backseat of your car before you left."

I'd baked the cookies for Aunt Hazel because Janice always brings my mother something. One of her melons in the summer, or a big bag of fresh kale in the fall, or in winter, some fresh-squeezed carrot juice.

"You should get your mother a juicer," said Janice, plunking a glass of carrot juice down by my plate. "Thanks," I said. (It's okay to say thank you for food.)

Janice's cropped wavy hair is gray, but her laugh is young, and when she says she's sixty I say, "Go on."

She's five feet tall if she stands on a piece of paper, with the sturdy build of a farmer, and I've never seen her in anything but jeans. Though she had to dress up for work all those thirty-three years of selling appliances for Baltimore Gas and Electric. Sold nineteen refrigerators one day, twenty TVs another. Won so many bonuses, hardly anybody in the family ever had to buy a freezer or a washer and dryer. And Aunt Hazel had enough kids for a baseball team.

A hip replacement slowed Janice down a few springs ago, but she literally crawled to the garden to put in the peas: "It was good for me." Besides, you can't buy Thomas Laxton peas, which have four or five peas to a pod, and freeze so well. She always puts up fifty-five bags. "So we'll have a mess of peas every week." And then some, for security.

She still mows the fields in the summer and stands on the tractor seat to pick persimmons off a tree planted years ago by some bird. "You got to wait until the first frost has sweetened them if you don't want your lips to pucker up like this," she told me, in a little puckery voice. Aunt Hazel shakes her head: What are we going to do with this girl?

We were having lunch in the big kitchen that has a rocker by the window that looks out on the cool, glassed-in porch where Janice keeps her cut flowers. "Look at those carnations still blooming," she said. "Your mother brought us those on Valentine's Day." You fill the vase up halfway with

Sprite, she said, and the stems take up the sugar. They'll last and last that way.

Have more tuna, she urged. More chips, more pickles. You can't drop by without eating. That would be rude.

"About not saying thank you . . . ," I said. (Trying to keep this family on course is like trying to plot out *The Double Life of Véronique*.) "My friend, Victor, never lets me say thank you for a plant, either, and he lives in Manhattan."

Aunt Hazel gave me a look. What kind of plants would grow in a place like New York City? I forged ahead. "Do you think that expression comes from the idea that the plants aren't really ours? You know, God made them, so we're just passing them on?"

"I don't know about that," Aunt Hazel said. Some people can just talk a thing to death.

Their farm is about two miles up the road from us. Take a left at the church, go past the cemetery, down the hill, across the stream, up another hill, and you're looking at a white house with a red roof and green shutters and the same locust trees that were there when the house was built in 1773. It's a rolling place; the cows used to wander from the big red barn down a path to the meadow by the stream that feeds a deep swimming hole we call Hickory Bottom. Its water still smells like leaves.

This is where Janice goes for her potting soil, taking humus from under the rotting logs.

If you think it's too early to plant greens, think again. Janice just rolls back some big old log lying near the south side of the house and scratches around in that rich earth underneath. Then she plants the seeds and leaves the log right where it is, to shelter the little bed from too much wind or sun. Then she sits on a chair made out of a locust stump and watches them grow. Just kidding.

We ate more pickles, which got us to talking cucumbers. Janice picked cukes every day last summer, even with the drought, thanks to a little watering system she rigged up with plastic milk jugs. She grows a cucumber plant in each corner of a five-foot-square bed, with a plastic jug sunk just up to its neck in the middle of the patch, which is mounded gently toward the center. The jug has one eight-penny nail hole poked in each corner, so that when you pour in water, it seeps slowly out toward the plant's roots.

"But I don't water them too much at first, because that forces a plant, and I think everything has its season," Janice said. "When the runners start, that's when I go out and fill my jugs up every evening." That's also when she mulches the whole patch with six to eight inches of clean straw, which keeps in moisture, and keeps the cukes cool. Never stop picking; it keeps them coming.

If you like pickles and want to keep a friend guessing: "Wait for a runner to flower and then stick it in a bottle," said Janice. "When the cucumber is a nice size, cut the runner off and put in vinegar and your sugar and spices and that's it. Everybody'll say, 'How did you do that?' "

When Cousin Helen Lee came to do Aunt Hazel's hair, I decided to go home and find a log. (Janice also told me how to keep raccoons out of the corn, but that's another story.)

I was already in the car when she ran out of the house. She handed a packet of Mexican sunflower seeds through the window. I didn't even say thank you.

Together at the Farm

Some friends came down to the farm on Preakness weekend to help me in the garden. They weren't like most people, who say they want to weed and then stand there asking if you have Ken Follett's *On Wings of Eagles* because Ross Perot says it tells everything we'd ever want to know about the corporate king who wants to be president.

It's hard to concentrate on the peppers when somebody like this is helping. You're likely to give the jalapeños an overdose of Epsom salts. You're liable to overreact (in the friend's opinion) when the friend sits down on your fluffy raised bed to discuss the abysmal state of the Democratic Party and then says: "Haven't you had enough of this now? Let's go into town."

But these people were like those Amish neighbors you see in movies who raise a barn and dance and sing and eat all in

one day. These people broke up soil the consistency of concrete; they trundled manure; they deadheaded scraggly old daffodils; they pulled up weeds without pulling up the clematis. They petted Molly the dog, and yelled at her just like family when she barked at Bernie, our Mr. Fix-It. (She loves to bark at Bernie because she knows how much he hates it.) They knew things from their own farm memories, I guess, about bringing out iced tea for the parched workers. They took walks without even asking directions. They'd go off in their car for a little jaunt and come back with tomatoes that had been vine-ripened in some hothouse somewhere, and deep red strawberries that called out for shortcake. (Sylvia makes the biscuit kind with plenty of butter and a dash of sugar.)

I'm not going to give out their full names because I don't want them to be invited to some better garden somewhere else to spend the weekend—where they can dig and sweat and wash dishes even more joyfully than at the farm.

They even knew how to make mint juleps. They had seconds of my rhubarb pie—*with* cream. They even brought books and disappeared upstairs at a gloriously early hour to read.

Last weekend, by contrast, the silence in my garden was deafening. I planted corn seed in mounds, the way the Wampanoags did a thousand years ago. I set out the Thessaloníki tomatoes I had started from a few seeds sent last winter by a fellow gardener in Pennsylvania. I planted the Brandywines a friend at work had given me, saying, "You have to try these because the catalog said they had that old-fashioned tomato taste." The plants were a little washed out from the hot ride down, so I gave them a drink of diluted fish emulsion and wondered if they'd make it through the week.

I was suddenly so alone with the tomatoes and my own thoughts that I felt like Olivia de Havilland before she goes bonkers in *The Snake Pit*. I wondered if Sylvia was baking her famous potato bread for Kim after hiking in the Pine Barrens out on Long Island. If Herbie was taking a luxurious drag on one of her unfiltered Camels and having a gin and tonic with a friend on her wide porch in Sea Cliff. If Cybele had planted all the plants we'd piled in her trunk after stuffing ourselves on her famous pasta with feta cheese and garlic and olives.

Some barn swallows swooped low over the garden catching their dinner of insects, and I thought of Herbie staring up into the walnut trees by the barn as we tried to identify the invisible bird chattering overhead. "They shouldn't make these trees so tall," she had said.

Kim might have known the bird, but we'd left him down by the stream poring over his wildflower book.

"He won't leave until he identifies that little yellow flower we thought was a buttercup," Sylvia had said. I used to think such behavior a bit obsessive—until Kim took a day and a half to dig around the roots of a cedar tree that had to be transplanted because it was in the way of my new kitchen garden. We thought he'd disappeared around lunchtime, but he was just in the hole, digging.

Bobby Bueller, who'd come to load some hay with his friend Dave, said sure, they'd help us heave the root ball into the wheelbarrow. So then we had to have a few beers, of course, and discuss the history of Bobby Bueller's hat and other fine hats we had known, and talk about our fathers who wouldn't throw anything away, not even an old rotten board, because as soon as you did you'd need it to fix the kitchen porch.

That's pretty much how a day goes around here. And it's hard to explain the enormity of it all to people who don't happen to share this particular obsession. They just look concerned (like maybe you should see a therapist) when you start talking about how coriander is supposed to repel the Colorado potato beetle, and that cosmos planted next to corn may deter the corn earworm.

"Isn't listening to Caribbean music on the harbor more exciting than hilling up the potatoes?" asked an acquaintance who'd urged me to drive into Baltimore on a perfect summer's evening.

Of course. Naturally. Gardeners *need* to get out of the garden now and then.

But try keeping up your end of the conversation with an independent filmmaker who's made an award-winning documentary about orgasms when your most intimate sexual thoughts have been, Could I plant the Rainbow Inca corn behind the barn so it won't be pollinated by the Silver Queen?

No, in May, planting-mania month, we gardeners are unfit for normal society.

But Sylvia thinks we're on to something. We might be able to get New Yorkers to pay good money, like they do at those rustic farms up in Vermont, for the privilege of rising at dawn to milk the cows. Only down here it's moving trees, mulching, digging more manure into that old Maryland clay.

A Plant Is Not an It

An iris likes to sit on the ground the way a duck sits on water: half in, half out.

"That's what the old-timers say," Cousin Bobby said. "Irises like sun on their rhizomes, so set them so they show through the soil."

I remember my first iris, wondering what to do with the knobby root that isn't a root at all, but a rhizome or stem that is planted horizontally just beneath the surface of the soil. Shoots grow up from this stem; the roots grow down. And somehow, I never felt very confident about setting it in the ground until the duck analogy.

We'd taken a ride over to Bobby's Maryland farm at the foot of Sugar Loaf Mountain to see his irises. He has 500 kinds (they're like potato chips, he says: you can't have just one), all in raised beds, each with an engraved metal tag.

Names like Loop the Loop (white with dark purple edges) and Spartan (deep red with chocolate overtones) and Touché (a beigy-lavender-bluish-violet affair that looks like Billie Holiday singing in a bar).

But even a silky deep purple beauty like Dusky Challenger has a hard time competing with a mountain. Sugar Loaf is like Maryland, more rounded than craggy, and the hills of Bobby's farm flow toward it like green waves. It's hard to do much else but look.

"When I moved in here twenty-five years ago, I knew this is where I'd spend the rest of my life," said Bobby, who spent thirty years as an extension agent for Montgomery County in Maryland. He's sixty years old and retired now, but he still keeps about twenty-five holsteins. (His cow Amy was grand champion at the state fair in 1974; she was like living art, Bobby says, just like his irises.) And even his big sister Janice, who's only a year older, says that Bobby's soil beats hers.

"It's the raised beds: he can till that soil with his hands," she said, staring at one of Bobby's favorites, Touch of Blue. It's like the sky on a clear day.

We had come to see the irises, but there were so many other distractions, like the deep pink and white lupines rising like flowered church steeples on the slope facing Sugar Loaf.

Come by in a week or two, Bobby said, when the seeds are ripe: "I'll give you some pods. All you have to do is roll them around in your hands and scatter the seeds." His voice drifted off as we watched a chimney swallow perched at the round door of her nesting box jab food into a number of pink gaping mouths.

"I want to see a bluebird," said my mother, with that same longing one feels when the smell of the ocean wafts into the car but you're still miles away.

I kept wandering back to the vegetable garden to have another look at the six great blue-green cabbages growing to perfection in a tiny four-by-five-foot raised bed, the hefty Vidalia onions, the mounds of bronze fennel that just keeps reseeding itself every year, the lovage that looks like a tree-size stalk of celery (put a few leaves in with the fresh trout when you're poaching it, Bobby says), the chamomile, which like the Johnny-jump-ups has turned into a welcome weed here.

It's not any one thing at Bobby's place that weaves the spell. It's everything together. Like learning how to put a little borage in with the chamomile when you make tea. Or how to set a few pieces of black rubber hose around the strawberry patch. They look like snakes, and the birds don't stop for berries. Janice taught him that.

There is a feeling of deep contentment emanating from this land and from Bobby, who, like Janice, was born a farmer and will die one.

"After I graduated from college, I came home to help Dad on the farm," he said. "But you know how it is when you have a lot of brothers and sisters, and they all have different ideas about the place. . . . Leaving was one of the hardest things I ever did."

But when you long for something, it may come to you in a different form. Bobby got a master's degree in agricultural economics in the early 1960s, when farmland was disappearing so fast the state was losing 10,000 acres a year. "Every morning at the extension office, we'd talk about what farm had caved in," he said.

A Plant Is Not an It

The speculators, to keep their taxes down—to farm levels—were asking farmers to farm the land they no longer owned. "I was a moonlighter, farming at night," he said. And he plowed the foot of Sugar Loaf for years, without knowing about the house. Then one day, deer hunting, he came upon it: A low-slung house with huge windows, lost in the brush.

"It was all grown up like a wilderness," he said. "The door was open, and the heat was on." A little foot trail led from the house to an old shack up on the hill. If you have only an outhouse, an unoccupied bathroom is irresistible.

Bobby moved in that winter and started bush-hogging the briars. And two years ago, when the investors put it up for sale, he bought the farm in cooperation with a land trust, so houses will never be built on these fields. Which is another reason for the deep contentment here.

But back to irises, which don't like fancy soil.

"I just went out with my bucket loader and took soil from the field and dumped it on top of the ground here," Bobby said. (You may not have a plain old field or a bucket loader, so just hold off on the aged manure.)

The beds are about eight inches deep, and the irises stand fifteen to eighteen inches apart.

"They do not want anything on those rhizomes except sun," Bobby said. "So keep the beds clean."

A little lime discourages rot disease, which sometimes attacks the rhizomes, especially if it's been rainy. But just scrape the rot out, he said, and soak the infected rhizome with a solution of one part bleach to ten parts water.

Irises are really very easy to grow, Bobby says, once you realize something. That a plant—or a cow like Amy—is not an "it" at all, but a Thou.

213

Memory and Myth

*T*he funny thing about the night the barn burned down is that none of us saw it happen. I mean no one who is still alive.

Grandmother Raver just told the story so well that it burned itself into the collective memory of our Maryland family, kind of like Heathcliff calling for Catherine on the moors in *Wuthering Heights*.

(Or did Catherine just imagine Heathcliff's voice? Or was it Catherine who called for Heathcliff? Or did Hollywood just make that up so that Laurence Olivier could roam the moors?)

See? Whatever really happens gets so changed by memory that the memory consumes the actual event.

. . .

I took in this foster child who always was a surly, ungrateful girl.
I think she was jealous of Salome, who also wasn't my own, but I
was partial to her and this girl knew it, and was always doing
things and blaming them on Salome. But we kept hoping she'd get
on better until that night.

This is the point where you would have to ask Grandmother, "Well? What happened?" and she would say, as she
crocheted to the beat of her rocker, "Oh, you don't want to
hear this old story," and you'd have to say: "Yes, I do. Tell
about the pump not starting."

Well, I woke up and the windows were all ablaze with light and
Carroll, Granddaddy Raver, was shouting at me, "Grace, start the
pump!" and all the men were running down to the barn to try to
get the animals out. And there I was in my nightgown and my
hair all down trying to start the pump with Carroll shouting,
"Start the pump! Start the pump!" and I was pumping and
pumping and no water was coming out.

Hours before, the girl had gone down to the barn and
opened up the spigots and just let the water run and run until
the pump went dry. Then she set the hay on fire.

Horses, you know, are so terrified by fire, they try to run back
into the flames.

Like the big horse my sister remembers that kept circling
about the field and galloping back to the door, where Aunt
Beulah stood flapping her white nightgown to scare him off.
He kept circling the field. I don't remember that at all. But
then, my older brother Carroll doesn't even remember the
girl.

After the fire, they found her (nobody can remember her
name) lying on her bed upstairs. She was the only one who
had not helped. And nobody remembers if she kept her si-

lence or confessed. But anyway, they took her back to Montrose, the home for delinquent girls.

(Montrose was the old Patterson mansion. *You remember,* Mother would say, as we drove by the lane of towering syc- amores, trying to make our ice cream cones last all the way home from town, *how Betsy Patterson married Jérôme, Napo- léon's youngest brother, but Napoléon never acknowledged their marriage and Betsy, who had a son, spent the rest of her life in Europe trying to establish their claim to the throne.*)

I'd think of the foster girl washing dishes in the old man- sion, thinking of starting another fire. I knew how Grand- mother played favorites and how mean she could be. How much hate would it take to burn a barn down?

This is a place as full of stories as of old roses, and if you are not careful, you can get lost in the past. I prune the mock orange bushes outside the kitchen window, listening to my mother and Cousin Janice laughing inside. I love the old house, but every piece of furniture seems set in its ways. Ev- ery room has its own memories—because so many other lives have been lived here. And when you are connected to them by blood they can suffocate you.

When you lie in the beds upstairs, no matter how indepen- dent you have become, there is always the danger of slipping back in a single instant into a child's world where you had to ask permission. And any newcomer is likely to be oppressed by ghosts—and the intricacies, for example, of just how a man should carve a country ham.

So I have been thinking about turning the old, rebuilt barn into a house—for me.

"Yeah, or a discothèque," a friend said, as we walked out of work one day, into the din of Times Square. Yeah. Some- thing to stir up the old ghosts. Even if it's just an old Bruce

Springsteen record, blasting out over the cornfields at two in the morning.

I left home when I was seventeen, and twenty-five years passed before I decided to come back to garden. But cabbages aren't the only things that need plenty of space.

One recent evening, we walked down to the barn with our coffee. It was a homey little delegation: my sister, Martha, and her husband, Rudy, my mother and I, my dog, Molly, and Mrs. Grey, the cat, bringing up the rear.

"Can't you just see a woodstove in the middle there?" Mother said.

"Or what about a big stone fireplace?" Martha said.

"Just walling off a third of this space would make a fine house," Rudy said.

"I'd put a porch in on the second floor, looking over the fields," I said. But inset, so it didn't ruin the lines.

We rolled open the door that looks out over the barnyard—where we used to pitch hay to the steers and soar, on our trapeze made of rope and an old wagon tree, over their knobby square heads.

That old hog house could be the greenhouse, Rudy said. And then we got to talking about the time Mr. Helwig got chewed up by the old sow.

He'd gone in to feed her and she turned on him and backed him up against the door. But Carroll heard him screaming and opened the door from the other side. Martha saw them coming up from the barn, the man leaning against the boy, blood streaming down his leg.

No, said Mother, your brother wasn't even there.

So it goes. Building new houses in a land of legend.

What Would Frank Say?

I knew the neighborhood was changing when Frank Fenbe's place turned into the Kitty Castle. Frank had a farm right next to ours, and his cows were always getting out into our pasture or the other way around, and his collie, Lassie, was always fighting with our boxer, Joe, and we'd crawl around in the bushes looking for them and drag them home to feed them aspirin water in their respective barns.

But Frank got old and his children didn't want the farm, so he and his wife, Catherine, moved to Wisconsin to be with their daughters and pretty soon his cornfields were cut up for house lots. The old house and barn and outbuildings remained, though, because a nice young couple from Reisterstown had moved in. They planted a big garden and kept up the old sour cherry trees and the grapevines, so nobody minded that their cats (a dozen or more—who counts in the country?) roamed the fields. Most cats around here were half wild anyway, because they were kept in the barn to catch rats. Sometimes we'd let Babyface in to thaw out on the radiator, but paying money to "board" a cat would have been sinful.

So now, every time we pass the Kitty Castle and see the red lights glowing through the trees, we wonder what Frank would say. The lights are just the infrared heat lamps that keep the cats warm on a cool night, but we suspect Frank might have seen them as yet another sign of the apocalypse. Cats in his hog house. Cats where his turkeys used to roost. Cats on couches where his hired man used to live.

Frank was a religious man, and he had taken on the rather hopeless task of trying to save our souls. He would come up on our kitchen porch in the summer and talk to my grandmother through the screened door as she had her soft-boiled eggs and coffee.

He'd tell her about the Day of Judgment as she dropped little pieces of white bread into her eggs and mushed it all together and said, "Frank, I have my religion and you have yours," and gave Joe the boxer the dregs of her coffee. Which was probably some kind of double sin, because stimulants were evil, and giving them to a dog had to be worse.

He must have known we were goners the evening he saw my mother raising her arms to the sky while she was out taking the clothes off the line. It was just yoga, but there was a full moon out and Frank must have thought it was devil worship, because he laid his head down on the hood of his tractor and started praying. I don't think he'd be too happy about the Kitty Castle.

But we are, because our own cat, Mrs. Grey, has stayed there twice, and it really is a castle. For two weeks, she got to eat her favorite food (Science Diet, for older cats, to keep her weight down), and her name was put up on the door of a big airy kennel that a Great Dane could live in comfortably for just about the rest of its life.

Every cat has a ledge to lounge on and a little basket with a pillow to sleep in and a chair to perch on if it wants to look out the big screened window, and a little door that leads to a sunny cat run that's bigger than a city patio. Fans keep the air circulating, the radio is turned to easy listening and the whole effect is sunny, yet cool.

"We tried air-conditioning but the cats hated it," said Pat Edel, who had a little plastic bonnet over her blond hair the day I dropped by, because she'd just been to the hairdresser and it was threatening to rain. "Dogs like to be cool, but cats like air and heat."

And if a summer's night gets a little chilly, on go those heat lamps: "The same way McDonald's heats up its french fries," Pat said.

Then she ran off to give a diabetic cat its insulin shot, and Kim shook his head over the love his wife pours on all these fur balls. (There was the time she drove one of her own cats 120 miles for an acupuncture session.) Their cats live in the converted shack where Frank's hired man used to live. They fixed it up with couches and a perch made out of a pine tree and added a cat porch after one of the new neighbors complained to the county game warden that a cat had been in his yard. Well, why didn't he just turn the hose on it, we say, but that's just it, see. Now we're supposed to have leashes on our dogs and locks on the doors and call before dropping by.

Anyway, somebody noticed what a cushy life these cats had and told Pat she should start a cat kennel.

"So I sat down one night and thought, What do my cats

like most? Sun, a little fresh air, enough room to move around in and a ledge to jump up on."

But it isn't just the palatial quarters or the fact that if the canned food is cold in the winter, it gets warmed up in the microwave oven. It's the attention. The Kitty Castle is like some great camp, where the youngsters come home singing campfire songs and begging for a horse.

But some cats never leave, because their owners abandon them to permanent camp. Or sometimes their owners go into a nursing home and never come back. And their old, failing cats live out their last years in the converted smokehouse, a kind of kitty hospice.

One time Pat and Kim spent thirteen nights crawling through Frank's old multiflora roses calling for a cat named Meow, who'd leaped from the arms of his owner. Is this excess? Would Frank have called it a sin?

It was Frank who was there the day I found Joe panting in the bushes with his stomach blown up like a balloon. I couldn't drive, so I ran over the hill and asked Frank to come quick in his Ford. He drove back up the hill at about five miles an hour, and we loaded Joe in the back and drove to the vet, the longest drive of my fifteen-year-old life, while Frank described my burning for eternity—unless I gave my life to the Lord. I told him I would if he'd drive a little faster. Joe died on the operating table, but I didn't blame Frank.

In a funny way, it seems right that the Kitty Castle is at Frank's place. The face of the neighborhood has changed, but the heart's still in the country.

Gardens of Steel
and Sky

*I*t was raining in my Maryland garden last weekend, so I decided to stay in New York and see what the city plants were up to. I've just moved into an apartment in the West Village, and I wanted to get a few moonflowers growing on my fire escape. I sit out there and watch the river in the mornings. But the view from the roof is the best. It's so good, I'm afraid somebody's going to take it away from me.

This is my garden in the city. I don't have any plants on the roof yet, and maybe I don't want any. The openness of sky and water is such a release, like running down to the very edge of the ocean. Just watching the clouds darken as the sun goes down over Jersey City and the ventilation pipes of the building next door blacken against the purplish sky is like being in a garden of a very different nature: a garden of space and movement that is free of clutter.

This is a garden of industry and commerce. The towers of

Wall Street lumber up into the clouds and disappear on foggy nights. And instead of watching herons on the river, I watch the cruisers go by. It's kind of a run-down block that everybody in the building fears will be gentrified. But for now—and some tenants have lived here for twenty years—it is comfortably unspiffy.

Nobody has many plants here because all the land has been covered with concrete. The only tree on the block is an ailanthus that seeded itself in a crack in the alleyway—in the exact spot where my air conditioner drips water from five flights up. This is the tree that grows in Brooklyn, of course, and everywhere else for that matter, poking its head up through grates and crumbling sidewalks and every vacant lot in the city.

Most people sneer at this tree. They say its leaves stink. They call it ugly. And it's true that there's nothing remarkable about its shape or color. But I admire its tenacity. It exhibits a bravery we all need to survive here. And like most New Yorkers, it's a transplant.

The tree of heaven, as ailanthus is commonly called, is native to China. It first made its way to England via a French Jesuit priest stationed in Beijing who sent some seeds to Phillip Miller, who planted them in the Chelsea Physic Garden in 1751. In 1784, William Hamilton planted the first saplings in America. Tree scholars ponder how this homely creature became known as the tree of heaven. For one thing, it shoots up to fifty or sixty feet in the blink of an eye. But for another, the name came from the Celestial Empire, the eighteenth-century name for that mysterious eastern land where the gods still walked in the mountains. And now, it lives happily among the poor.

I was thinking these things as I took a kind of busman's

holiday from my garden. I decided to walk to Battery Park and set off down West Street, past its landscape of parking lots and chain-link fences and discarded tires. Just south of Chambers Street, I noticed another ailanthus, a sixty-footer, growing next to an old four-story brick building on the corner of an abandoned lot. The building's first floor looked like a garage, its steel doors covered with graffiti; the windows above were so full of soot, it would be hard for anyone living there even to look out.

It's one of those lone, derelict houses you see on the edge of nowhere, the ones left standing for some reason after everything else on the block was sliced away for some redevelopment project that never developed.

Farther south, I passed another field full of Queen Anne's lace and reeds, goldenrod and lamb's-quarter and I wanted to walk through it, but a chain-link fence kept me out. Two enormous old beams—one tilted against the other—lay in the field like the crumbling remains of a shipwreck. I thought it a fine sculpture for the city. And in the movement of the tall grasses, I felt the sea and remembered that Manhattan was once a wild island reached only by canoe.

Then I came to civilization: Hudson River Park, where there are curving walkways bordered by neat plantings of daylilies and astilbe and viburnum and artemesia, and I immediately missed the unruliness I had left behind. We need parks, of course—safe places for people to read and walk in, where children can run on the grass—but I wish that they reflected more of our conflicting nature.

I was happy to see pine and beach roses and grasses planted along the shore—those rugged plants that grow wild on the dunes of blustery Montauk, Long Island—but I want more of them. And more hawthorn and crab apple and Russian olive.

And why not a field of sunflowers for children to run through, instead of closely clipped lawns? Why not paths of sand or crushed oyster shells winding through a quarter acre of black-eyed Susans and Queen Anne's lace? In a time when cities can't afford to pour money and water on plants, why not embrace the ones as hardy as ailanthus? Less tidy plants that would give us a break from our tight, controlled city lives. These perennial beds make me so uncomfortable.

By now, I was in Battery Park City, where I am always struck by the power of steel and glass on one side and the primeval flow of the tide on the other. I sat down in a deserted section of an outdoor café—the tables were spattered with rain—to have lunch near the yachts moored by the World Financial Center. I thought of all the gardeners in their gardens, pulling weeds and battling bugs—and how we make ourselves prisoners there.

A little sparrow perched himself on the back of a nearby chair. "Chirp, chirp, chirp," he said, staring right at me. I've never been so close to a bird.

"Chirp, chirp, chirp," he repeated. I started to get all gushy about nature in this landscape of steel. Until I realized what he wanted: "Give me a corn chip!"

I ended up breaking bread with a flock of sparrows. But I drew the line at the frozen margarita.

It was good to get out of my garden—and into a bigger one that defies all boundaries.

Of the Land

I live in Manhattan now. A lot of country children do. They can't wait to leave all that manure and the land of Sunday school pins and *Reader's Digest*s piled in the bathrooms. They tend to choose the biggest cities they can find, needing a powerful antidote to the provinces.

In the low-rise streets of Greenwich Village, I still drink espresso as greedily as someone coming off Maxwell House for the first time, and good crusty prosciutto bread as if Italy were about to vanish from Prince Street. I have discovered how much cheaper films are than therapy, and I don't think I will ever tire of just walking, still put pleasantly off balance by the people I see, because they just don't act this way where I come from.

Yet I can't seem to yank my roots from the Maryland farm that has been in my family for four generations, ever since

Of the Land

1870 when my great-grandfather John Franklin Raver, a
stocky farmer who lived a few miles to the east, walked
through the woods and laid eyes on Mary Elizabeth Bond, a
young woman of seventeen, whose father still held 450 acres
of the original 1761 land grant from Lord Baltimore.

Mary and John settled down in a log house by a cold running spring on the farm to have thirteen children. Until
Mary got tired and died at thirty-seven. When John Franklin
died, the land was offered to the children, and my grandparents, young newlyweds then, bought 120 acres—the same
hills I wander now.

For two centuries, fields of corn and soybeans and rye have
crisscrossed these hills in an orderly patchwork. I realized the
other day, digging a bed for a late shipment of lilies, why I
always think of vegetables when someone says "garden."
Green-blue kale. Fat heads of broccoli. Sweet carrots. Corn
ripped from the stalk and thrown into the boiling pot.

Farmers connect the earth to sustenance. They plant crops
first. Then trees to mark their land, to shade the house and
shelter it from wind. Flowers come later, when there is time
to feed the soul.

My father died in April, after I watched his fiery temper
fade for many months. It wasn't a surprise, but losing a
father—the patriarch—is a shock you can't prepare for. Suddenly there is this empty space where once a man shouted
and laughed—a void, regardless of how good or bad your relationship was.

When my father died, I had the distinct, almost visual
sensation of his energy going up and away in a whirling gyre.
Where is this person, I kept asking myself, as we rang the
bell for him up at the old church, as we carried his polished

cherry coffin into the graveyard that holds the bones of his mother and father and his mother's mother and father and his mother's grandparents.

The succession of names in the cemetery and on the stained glass windows is like an incantation: Leave this place and these ghosts and the incurious faces of the people who stayed.

So I did. And by now I have lived in many cities.

And then one day in Missouri I rode over a pasture in a beat-up Ford with a farmer who wanted me to see his cows. I was stuffed full of home-cured bacon and fresh eggs from the breakfast he'd made in the house his father built.

"Most people can't wait to leave home," he said, as the truck stalled in a grassy ravine. "And then they spend the rest of their life trying to get home."

It's just the story of Oedipus, I guess, though some sons don't have to kill their fathers and marry their mothers and blind themselves to come into their own.

And what about the daughters? How do they find their true selves in a family where the father was king?

The men in my family got their land from the women, who then bore them children, who then thought of the land as their fathers' land.

Yet it was my Grandmother Grace, who wasn't a Raver at all, who seared herself into my memory with her gritty humor and her outrageous egotism, and the stories that she painted in her dark wallpapered room. They were as real to me as the very night the barn burned down.

Their faces stare out of the old velvet albums with stern expressions and fantastic hairdos, their arms resting on fake pillars. Grace is shown as a skinny bride in glasses with an ornate comb sticking straight out of her head. A few years later, she stands like a stout ship next to her wiry husband, Carroll, whose hands, my oldest brother says, were like iron.

Now my mother lives there alone. It is her home now, though she came from a little town on the Eastern Shore, never dreaming she'd have to chop off a chicken's head if Sunday dinner was ever going to get on the table. Now these fields and these views from every window are hers, and they are what she wants to look out on the day she dies.

We all talk carefully about what will happen to the farm, about who, if any of us, could carry on the stewardship of the land, with our lives so far afield from the potatoes we used to dig behind the barn.

In the evenings, I look out over the twinkling lights of the suburban houses that cropped up when the first neighboring farmer got old and his children didn't want the place. They have green useless lawns where corn and wheat once grew, and neo-colonial pillars pretending to hold up plantations. Yet I like some of the people who live in them. Especially our neighbor across the road, who shot a buck in our woods and insisted on hanging its small head, Teddy Roosevelt–style, over his mantel.

I have decided to garden down in Maryland this year, grabbing long weekends, even weeks when I can, if my computer and I can keep the copy flowing to New York. I know a lot of people who live like this these days. People like me, who get hooked on the city, but can't shake the clay off their feet.

Still, it seems a strange way to live. Not to have your coffeepot in one place. Not to watch the bugs and the birds and the snap peas every day. I could do that in New Jersey, I guess. But I can't seem to turn my back on this rolling land.

There's an old stone foundation near the barn that once

supported a house for guinea hens. The roof caved in years ago, but the stones, gathered a century ago from the fields, are solid. Maybe I'll build a cottage there, with a porch, to take in the fields, the very sweep of which poses the old question: Can you go home again?

Make an old place new? Coax friends from New York to come down with a little pasta and espresso and the overwhelming desire to weed? Get to know the people back home, who could teach me plenty?

I don't know. But maybe a year of digging and planting and pruning the old moss roses Grandmother brought from her mother's house will hold the answers.

A Patio That
Girls Built

One nice warm day last May, Annamaria Rossetto couldn't get her chaise longue to behave itself. She'd placed it on the little lawn (well, let's call it a hill of indigenous undergrowth) outside her apartment in Thomaston, and it kept sort of toppling this way and that.

It's hard to read and sip wine when you're listing at a 30-degree angle. Her friend Pamela Schider, sipping wine, said, "Time to build a patio, Annamaria. It'll be great. Build a little rock garden while we're at it."

So they did. Two girls, as the men at the hardware store say. Whatchu want with that thing? they kept asking, every time the girls dropped by for some new thingamajig they needed. You ever do this before? Better get somebody to do it for you. Somebody meant a man.

Well, Rossetto and Schider (who met in a karate class) would just give these guys a level look (you need a level to build a patio) and take off down the aisles to find the thing-amajig, and when they came across it, they'd bring it back to the counter, plunk it down and haul out their dough.

That way, you get what you need. If you come in—all the contractors standing around shooting the breeze—and start asking, "How do you . . . ?" like a girl asking Daddy to un-screw a jar lid, somebody'll say, "Where's your husband?" and all the contractors will go ahead of you.

How many of you out there (not any of you big men) have wanted to build something like this in your gardens and been discouraged (even in this liberated day) by some kind of "poor little ol' you" remark?

Well, Rossetto and Schider want to just say—as they lean back in their well-behaved chairs on their lovely patio—what a lot of men won't: It's easy, girls. Anybody with a few brains and a couple of muscles can build one.

Here's how they did it.

"The first thing you have to do is think about it," said Rossetto.

Now this sounds like an obvious piece of advice, but how many of us have gone into a project half cocked, and ended up looking silly at the hardware store? Not to mention spending a lot of money on the wrong thing. Or botching the project so badly we start looking for our husbands. And for some people, that could delay the project indefinitely.

Rossetto will be the first to admit her own silly mistakes. "I thought at first you could just lay some tiles down on the ground," she laughed. "But the chair wouldn't sit up straight on those, either, of course, because of the hill."

Rossetto spent about a solid week planning the project. She decided she wanted a simple eight-foot-square patio made of railroad ties and black and red clay tiles. A sort of chessboard effect, big enough for a few chairs and a barbecue.

She made a sketch, figured out how many ties she needed, how many spikes to nail them together, what kind of tiles and how many, that sort of thing.

Then, she let her fingers do the walking.

"Whenever you do anything in life, your best friend [she didn't say a girl's best friend] is the telephone book," said Rossetto. "I just called everybody to get the best price on supplies."

And there's quite a difference. Railroad ties, for instance, varied from $11 to $18, depending on the number ordered and whether you want delivery. (They must be pressurized, too, not waterproofed with creosote, which is injurious to plants.)

Pam Schider actually had a little experience—she'd helped her husband build a retaining wall, so she had a feel for what the project entailed. But she doesn't make a profession out of calluses—she's a social worker at a nursing home. Rossetto plays piano at the Tung Ting in Centerport.

The main challenge, of course, was to construct a level surface on a hill that rises about 30 degrees from the street. That meant—if you can picture this—that the railroad tie nearest the house would be the high point, and Rossetto and Schider would have to build the rest of the patio up to meet that first tie.

Now this may not be the kosher way to do it—they didn't consult any how-to books on the subject—but they simply set the first railroad tie into the top of the hill, then placed the left-hand tie at right angles to the first, propped it up temporarily with bricks and began to clear the site.

"We used pickaxes and shovels to get rid of the under-growth," said Schider. "Then we had to fill in with extra soil to build the hill up."

That took two truckloads—they borrowed Schider's husband's 1965 Chevy pickup—of subsoil from a nearby construction site. A man on an earth mover watched them in amusement and then said, as they finished shoveling the second load, "You know, girls, that isn't topsoil."

Rossetto and Schider weren't stealing topsoil for their geraniums. But they pretended to be real disappointed at their silly mistake—just to make him feel good. Then they slammed the door of the truck and took off with the subsoil.

As they placed the ties to form a box, they kept fine-tuning with a carpenter's level to make sure they'd end up with a horizontal plane—not a patio that listed so the guests would spill their wine.

They used twelve-inch spikes to connect the railroad ties at the corners, nailing them in on the diagonal with a sledge-hammer. A male passerby shook his head in amazement. But Rossetto and Schider still shake *their* heads in amazement—that it really doesn't take all that much muscle. Once the ties were in place, they filled the "box" to about six inches from the top, then added a layer of sand. It's easier to place tiles on sand than soil.

"The tiles are going to settle at different levels, and with sand, you can just lift up the end of a tile and add some here and there—sort of like icing a cake," Rossetto explained. "You couldn't do that with soil very well."

So they had to go buy a yard and a half of sand, which isn't like buying silk, girls. It's measured by the scoop, and just why it's called yard must have something to do with boy talk.

But anyway, they needed a scoop and a half, which means they bought a yard and a half and trucked it home.

By now, the neighbors were starting to get impressed. The man across the street asked Schider if she were for hire—he needed a gardener and a maid, all in one.

Schider, tamping the tiles down with a tamper (she describes it as a big wooden block attached to a long handle that's so heavy it must be filled with concrete), said thank you very much, but no.

They broke a few tiles, by the way, which is a good reason for getting extras. And they also had to forget their dream of a chessboard (Rossetto's landlord was actually going to make some giant chess figures), because they goofed on the number of squares—fifty-six instead of sixty-four.

But why sweat the small stuff? It took them about three days of hard work, but Rossetto got a lovely little patio for $700.

"I think it would have cost about $2,000 if I'd had it done," said Rossetto, placing her wineglass on a little table that sat perfectly level.

Not to mention the plantings that Schider made around the edges—periwinkle and narcissus, hostas and ferns, some nice round rocks she brought over from her home in Huntington.

Rossetto put her leg up—she's recovering from a little karate accident—and sighed contentedly.

"The great thing about our patio," she said, "is that when people get near it, they want to be *on* it. They can't bear to stand down on the street."

And now, when the two girls go into the hardware store, they know they've become one of the boys.

"The other day the guy showed me this thing that's like

the head of a screwdriver," said Schider. "I don't know what it's called, but you put this thing in your drill and set the screw in it and drill the hole and screw the screw all at the same time."

The guy had said, "Here, use this. It only costs ninety-five cents. That's what the contractors all use. Nobody uses nails anymore."

Well, nobody except a girl, maybe. And if somebody would just tell her about this new thingamajig, she could be a contractor.

Defying Beetles

When my father went into the hospital last summer, the Japanese beetles decimated his roses. It was almost obscene how much they enjoyed themselves, mating on the deep green leaves, burrowing into the blossoms.

Where before nary a leaf on a hundred plants had black spot or powdery mildew, now all seemed blighted. Where a mass of pale pink, creamy white, fiery orange and deep velvety red had bloomed in front of the hollyhocks by the old henhouse, and marched down the side of the old lilac bushes (my father, the son of a farmer, couldn't get out of straight lines), there now stood a wasteland of skeletonized leaves.

When a gardener grows ill, the garden begins to die, as if some dwindling life force first shuts off there.

Each night, my mother would return from the hospital and say: "He's doing better today. He'll be out in a few days."

We grown children, back in Maryland for an emergency

visit, would nod, pour her a little scotch and say nothing about the empty space on the table where roses had always spilled out of a silver basket.

One evening Bernie came to the door. He's the man who mows the grass, fixes machinery, sprays the roses. My father, by then kept alive by IVs and rarefied air, believed in miracle drugs. And he sprayed his roses—or rather, had Bernie spray—with the same faith. Benlate for black spot and powdery mildew, Malathion for aphids and leafhoppers and thrips and beetles and any other living thing unlucky enough to cross the path of lethal chemicals.

The roses were beautiful. They had that strange smell of rose spray, and their leaves were sometimes still dusty with the poison, but to my father this was no more avoidable than the swollen feet or stomach trouble that resulted from all the pills colliding in his own chemistry.

"Have you ever seen anything as deep a red?" he would say as he cut a big bloom off Chrysler Imperial, a rose that has everything but whitewall tires. And what a dark, beautiful crimson it was, like plush upholstery just this side of excess.

My father loved intricate, passionate things. The Bach double violin concerto. *Carmina Burana.* The unfolding of a rose that went from pink to white in the sun. His children, when they excelled.

In later years, I would follow him about the garden with a coffee can of hot water as he chose the best roses for the table.

"Cut just above those five leaves," he would say, always the teacher. His hands trembled toward the end, and his feet wavered over the grass as if we were crossing an uncertain sea. When the can was full I would take them down into the cool cellar, where they would open up like a man's secret heart.

I had never tried to grow hybrid teas myself. They're pampered creatures, which easily succumb to insects and disease. The old climbers and species roses can thrive without chemicals, but a rose like fiery Tropicana or the elegant pink Tiffany seems to wilt at the very thought of survival without the arsenal of nerve poisons and fungicides in the shed. Some of my father's old canisters probably contained the last DDT in the county, his children joked.

But they were not a joke to Bernie, who had to spray every ten days, when Dad was keeping count. He would feel nauseated, lightheaded; he would get short of breath. But it would go away. And the roses were so beautiful.

But Bernie had some health problems of his own that summer. And nobody else had the time—or the inclination—to spray. So here was a rose ghost land, populated by beetles.

"Let them die," said my father, a perfectionist. "They're no good to anyone like that."

The children looked at one another across his bed, and later that day stopped off at the garden center. Rudy reached for the Malathion. I grabbed a bottle of Benlate. Bernie went into action again.

By October, roses filled the house again. And my father lived for another six months.

In April, the leaves came out bushy and green. But the ground had shifted.

"I'd like to keep them going," my mother said one morning as magnolia blossoms floated to the ground. "But I hate to think of Bernie using that sprayer."

And as in many moments to come, she and I looked at each other, timid navigators charting new territory.

"Well, we could try to grow them organically," I said. "If the Brooklyn Botanic Garden can do it, why can't we?"

"Why not?" said Mother.

No argument from Bernie.

And so we tried. First battling the aphids, those little green insects that suck the life out of tender buds. Every night my mother would drag the 100-foot hose out to the rose beds and spray them full force.

"Well, it discouraged them, but they're still there," she'd report on the phone to New York.

So we went into phase two: Safer's insecticidal soap. When you're brought up on Sevin, it's hard to believe that plain water works. A little Safer's in a plastic bottle engenders more faith.

All spring and summer the reports and suggestions flowed back and forth on the telephone. There were a few holes here and there, but the roses were blooming. There was a bit of black spot, but the bicarbonate of soda was keeping it down. The bees were swarming over the hollyhocks. Bernie felt just fine. And the roses smelled like roses.

Then the heat wave struck, and the beetles crawled out of the ground, like hordes sent by Yahweh to test our faith. When I visited my mother in July, the air was buzzing with them. They covered the blossoms of every bush. They clung to the purple flowers of the chaste bush. They got in my hair as I hung up the wash. They flew down my shirt.

The rose beds are a graveyard again. There was something horrible about leaving such fragile creatures to the wild. Like setting out virgins for vampires.

"So maybe we'll have to take them out," I said. "Grow ramblers or climbers instead."

"Well, I think we should put some milky spore down," my mother said.

I said yes. I said we should try again next summer. But I

241

am my father's daughter. In my heart I can't believe these creatures will grow without an arsenal of Du Pont and Ciba-Geigy backing them up.

But my mother just called. She has a lead on horse manure. So I'm going down to dig it in, aerate the heavy Maryland soil, maybe pull out a few weaklings. Then we'll see what June brings.

Heroic Bagworms

The bagworms must have started eating the cedar trees the summer my father was sick—too sick to notice or care. Or maybe he cared, but he could not muster the energy to do anything about it.

They ate their way through the summer, suspended in strange little silk bags covered with twigs and leaves. Then, in September, they laid millions of eggs.

We didn't know any of this then. That such incredible progeny—and its destruction—was proceeding so smoothly, while inside the house a man fought for air and considered his life.

Sometimes I would look into his eyes and see fear there and have to look away, because it is so hard to imagine death. My father did not believe in heaven. He believed in physical matter, in molecules.

Last spring, the spring my father died, millions of tiny bag-worms emerged from their mother's silk purses and were blown by the wind on their own silk threads to other trees, to begin feeding on the bark and leaves.

By summer, they had skeletonized two of the fourteen-foot red cedars that my father had brought as seedlings years ago from our swampy woods.

"We really should do something about the trees," my mother said, as we both stared at the brown, brittle branches. "Do you think they'll live?"

Somehow, neither of us could deal with it. We were wait-ing for a man to take charge. Get out the spray gun and nuke them with something we would not question because this was man's work. Or fire up the chain saw and cut the trees down. Burn the infested wood in the old concrete-block incinerator. We let it go.

By last fall, the bagworms had spread to the taller cedar. And last week, we eyed the thirty-foot spruces nearby.

We stood there teetering, wishing they would just go away but knowing we had to do something to stop them. Finally, I dropped by my county cooperative extension office, which advises farmers and gardeners on everything from corn seed to compost.

"Cut off the bags and destroy them," said Bill Sacks, one of the master gardeners on duty that day.

I told him how high up they were.

"Well then, you have to wait until the eggs hatch in early June and spray with Orthene," he said.

But I don't use pesticides.

"Oh, well, in that case, soapy water will kill them," Mr. Sacks said. "Or Bt, but you have to wait a few days."

"Yeah," said another master gardener, Joe Turner, shaking his head. "You don't get the satisfaction of a good clean hit like you do with Orthene."

Bt, or *Bacillus thuringiensis*, is a bacterial species that acts as a stomach poison for certain susceptible caterpillars—the younger, the better. A newly hatched bagworm, for instance, feeding on the leaves of a cedar sprayed with Bt stops eating and dies.

Orthene, the brand name for acephate, is both a contact spray and a systemic organophosphate that acts as a nerve poison. If it doesn't kill the caterpillar on contact, it may be absorbed by the roots of the tree and hits the insect again when it feeds on the plant's leaves.

It is toxic to bees and birds, and is classified as a possible human carcinogen. And it is readily available to the home gardener to spray on bagworms.

"But soapy water will work fine, too," Mr. Sacks said. "Safer's, or good old Murphy's soap. Mix two tablespoons of Murphy's with a gallon of water and add two table-spoons of rubbing alcohol."

The mixture simply dries up the cuticle membrane of a soft-bodied insect and it dies.

So why not recommend it in the first place?

Mr. Sacks shrugged: "Most people don't want to wait. With the soap, you have to know a little bit about the insect. Wait for them to hatch out around Memorial Day."

To hear an entomologist talk about a bagworm is almost to love one. The eggs spend the winter in their mother's silk bag and when they hatch around Memorial Day, they emerge through a little hole in the bottom and are dispersed by the wind.

"They balloon on long threads of silk, which they generate, and the silk acts like a drag, pulling them through the air to another host," said John Neal, a federal entomologist in Beltsville, Maryland.

No bigger than grains of pepper, they begin to chew on the plant's woody stem and then its leaves, spinning their own silk bags around themselves, covering them with bits of twigs and leaves. When it molts—six or seven times during the summer—the bagworm parks itself on a stem, ducks down into its bag and sheds its skin, tossing the old one out the top of the bag.

"It's a litterbug, but you've got to do something with the skin," said Dr. Neal, defending his worm.

By summer's end, the bags are about one and a half inches long, and the caterpillars, which have now turned upside down, pupate into moths.

After a pheromone is secreted by the female, the male flies to his mate. Then the poor fellow has to insert his abdomen, while hanging upside down, into the bottom of the female's silk bag. After this heroic feat, he flies off and dies, never having seen his mate.

In three or four days, the female emerges from her pupal case and deposits her eggs.

"She is a wisp of herself," Dr. Neal said. "She dies either inside and falls to the bottom of the bag or drops out the bottom and the ants take her away."

I dug out the Murphy and considered the tragic life of the bagworm. And I wished Dad were around. "Oh, go on," he'd say. "Just use some Orthene."

Beyond the Garden

I have flirted with my family's farm in Maryland all summer. And now, as the nights fall earlier and the lightning bugs no longer flash in the velvety air between the house and barn, it sits there like a person asking quietly: "Well? What now?"

When I went down to garden there this past spring—grabbing weekends and scraps of weeks when I could—I had a lot of romantic ideas of how I would carry on the farm that has been in our family for four generations. Maybe an herb farm, organic vegetables, perennials for the suburbanites, an artists' colony, a summer camp, a gardening school, a nature preserve. I was full of nostalgia, too, for those summer childhood days of wading in the stream and building little dams with rocks, of crawling through tunnels of hay, of digging up potatoes in the hot dusty field behind the barn.

But I have grown tired of that voice sunk in the past. And my rosy fantasies are bumping up against reality.

Just west of our little country road—already dotted with suburban houses—is an old 500-acre farm that nestles in a little valley bordered by the Patapsco River in Carroll County. You get there by walking down a steep gravel road through a woods filled with ferns and oak trees, dogwoods and black locusts. But now red surveyor flags—for a 127-lot subdivision and an eighteen-hole golf course—dot the once-productive orchard, the old fields of corn and wheat, the pastures where horses once grazed.

If I were in the city, all of this could remain an abstraction, just one more example of old unwanted farms being eaten up by suburban sprawl. But when you get to know a place— where the deer lie down at night, how the fields curve around a stand of black walnut trees or where the Turk's-cap lilies bloom by the stream—it becomes a personal, painful matter. And it forces one to ask, "What am I, as an individual, going to do about preserving the land?"

It also makes me wonder how other people think about land. Will they wonder what was there before, when they move into their half-million-dollar house with a fairway rolling past the lawn? I don't think so. People moving from the city—or, more likely, from older suburbs with smaller lots and smaller houses—probably don't have any memory of the country. They never ran down the rows of high corn or sneaked through the meadow when the bull was out. They grew up in houses with an attached garage, in the middle of a lawn with some azalea bushes and a flowering tree, set on a well-lighted street. So they take that vision with them.

I know everybody deserves a little green space, but where are we going to grow the wheat and corn and beans if the

golf courses keep replacing the fields? And it isn't just the rain forests that are losing birds and animals and wild plants to the bulldozers. You hear this refrain so often that it sounds like a cliché. But only because we turn such deaf ears to an obvious truth.

I've had to face up to something else this summer: commercial agriculture's dependency on pesticides. I never noticed before—though I'm sure it's been going on for decades—the fields of brown, dead vegetation that alternate with the young emerald fields of wheat in the spring. What is wrong with those fields, I asked myself as I drove down from New York in April. Then I realized the fields had all been sprayed with herbicides. When farmers use weed killers, they don't have to till—seeds are simply planted in tiny holes drilled between the rows of the last crop—and the practice cuts down on erosion. But chemical residues build up in the soil, and billions of microbes are lost.

Later this summer, as I was showing off the butterflies and bees in my organic garden, a helicopter rattled into the sky, spraying the surrounding fields with a white dust that made our throats tighten up. I found out later that it was methomyl, a broad-spectrum insecticide commonly used on string beans.

There are less toxic insecticides, but farmers say that their yields would be smaller, the beans less perfect. And in a competitive field where all the other farmers are using the same kind of chemicals, it is difficult to reverse the trend.

Last year, I would have leaped on my organic soapbox, decrying the farmers. But until I, personally, can prove that alternatives work, it's just empty talk to cast aspersions on the men and women who have farmed there for generations— and who love the land, too.

Living on a piece of earth is like entering into a relationship with another person. It's easy to make declarations of love. But it's hard work getting to know someone—or a place—in a real way that faces up to all the things you never guessed were there. How could you, before you rolled up your sleeves and got to work with the rest of the imperfect people who do things like use pesticides and, maybe even golf?

This year, my mother put in a new septic tank and replaced the roof of the smokehouse. Then the roof over the kitchen started to leak. Then the pump stopped drawing water from the well for some reason. It was the old pipes, she discovered, that had to be replaced. Now the old riding mower is making noises. This is the real life of a person trying to hold on to a farm full of memories.

There are no road maps for these territories. I walk down the lane past the barn and wonder how to tackle the poison ivy that climbs twenty feet into the black walnuts. We can't even get to the stream anymore without loppers to cut down the briars. The woods beyond the stream are a tangle of honeysuckle and brambles. We need to take inventory of the trees and native plants, open them up to light and air.

When you move forward, the memories fade, because you are chopping your way into the unknown future. Next spring, my garden—the tomatoes and flowers, that is—will be simpler. Because it is the larger garden—the fields and the woods—that I need to know now.

Horseshoes and
Humility

*L*ooking into the life of a primitive animal can shed a little light on the so-called higher species.

Take the horseshoe crab, for instance, which is actually
more closely related to a spider than a crab, but somebody
apparently thought it looked like a horseshoe and mistook its
pincers for crab legs. I myself think it looks more like a hel-
met plowing the sand.

I've grown fond of these creatures roaming the beaches,
and one wintry day I asked myself, like Holden Caulfield
wondering about the ducks, where all the horseshoe crabs go
in the winter. In April they come up on the beach to mate.
In June they hang out in the shallows, feeding on worms and
clams. In the fall their cast-off shells lie heaped among the
seaweed like the discarded armor of some ancient race.

But come winter, where do they go? Out, that's all.

Into the deeper waters off the continental shelf, where

temperatures hover in the fifties and nobody freezes, but nobody gets all that comfortable either. Like in the 1970s, when we turned our thermostats down to 68 and wore those dopey-looking booties on our feet.

This galumphy-looking American horseshoe crab, *Limulus polyphemus*, has survived 360 million years, if you count the arthropod's forebears. *Limulus* can boast only 60 million years, but that's not bad considering *Homo sapiens* has only been around for 300,000 years. And *Homo erectus*, our first relative, first stood up only 1.5 million years ago. Which is like being a newborn if you're a horseshoe crab.

If you've seen the continents shift and mountains rise out of the sea and dinosaurs come and go, you take the long view on life. You're a survivor, like the cockroach.

So how come they've hung in there, while most others have fallen by the wayside of the evolutionary road?

"Well, there have always been oceans, and there have always been sandy beaches, so there's always been a habitat for them," said Robert Loveland, a biologist at Rutgers University. (Keep that in mind when the recession forces you into a one-room apartment.)

Way back in the Cretaceous period, a giant sea went clear around the world. Then the glaciers formed, and the continents started to move, and America drifted eastward, the horseshoe crab drifting with it. Today *Limulus* makes its home from the Yucatán Peninsula to Wiscasset, Maine. Which is another reason I like this crab. It isn't a West Coast surfer type.

In short, this animal is flexible. It cruises the sandy bottoms of icy Maine, it basks in the balmy blue seas off the Yucatán. It bathes in salt and brackish water alike. It is not a picky eater but happily composts clams, worms, fish, crabs, fishing line. Which is a big advantage in the food web, and brats who whine about eating their lima beans should take heed. If you eat everything on your plate, you won't disappear when the roast beef does.

There are many parallels to be drawn between *Limulus* and us, but one entrancing difference is the plight of the male during the mating ritual: not enough females to go around. So those males who do hook up with a female, hang on, literally, for dear life. Now there's a switch for you.

The matchmaking takes place in the water, where the male—who is refreshingly smaller than the female—clambers onto her back and clasps his hooklike claws about her shell. There he hangs, for days, weeks, even months.

Which makes perfect sense in a world where there's only one female to every three males. "It's kind of like, 'Hey, I've got one already, why play the field,' " said biologist Mark Botton of Fordham University at Lincoln Center. Botton and Loveland should know. They spend more time in Delaware Bay—horseshoe crab heaven—than Darwin did in the Galápagos stalking the rhinoceros iguana.

And they've observed some rather brilliant behavior in a supposedly dumb animal. During mating season, for instance, the female comes ashore—male clasped to her back—on the highest tides of the year. She digs a hole at the water's edge and lays about 4,000 eggs, in a cluster no bigger than a golf ball, while a bunch of "suitor," or unattached, males try to push off her mate and fertilize the eggs themselves. Sound familiar? When the tide ebbs, she goes back into the sea, male still on her back, to wait for the next high tide, when she will return to lay 4,000 more eggs.

These eggs, buried in the sand by the full moon's high tide mark, will be safe for two weeks, until the new moon appears and pulls the water up once more to the nests. Then the trilobites—horseshoe crab babies—hatch from their shells and swirl out into the foamy sea. Most are preyed upon by fish, but since every female produces about 300,000 youngsters a year, that's just nature's way of feeding her other offspring.

Speaking of which, the humble horseshoe crab may well be responsible for keeping songbirds alive. In the spring, thousands of warblers and ruddy turnstones migrate from South America to the Arctic Circle to breed. And though a ruddy turnstone may be a shadow of his former self when he drops down, after a nonstop flight from Suriname, enough crab eggs, and he flies right on to Hudson Bay.

It just goes to show how you can go along for years— millions, for some species—with no great purpose in life. You may feel you're doing nothing more than bulldozing the murky bottoms of dark seas, keeping the kids in shoes and peanut butter. You may think, fleetingly, of dreams you once had. Of painting a beautiful picture or changing, somehow, the very consciousness of the world. You may even wish, now and then, that this guy would get off your back. (What's for dinner, hon?)

But hey, learn from *Limulus*. She just goes along until a big wave knocks him off. And everybody goes their separate ways. Until spring. When they give it another whirl.

Wasteland

*I*t's amazing how we can get used to anything. Here we are living right by some of the most beautiful beaches in the world, and we're afraid to swim in the water.

It's the kind of thing I used to read as a kid in my *Weekly Reader*. It was usually some country behind the Iron Curtain, or some undeveloped country being raped by some developed one, like us, only the *Weekly Reader* never gave that lesson. "Imagine having to drink bottled water," I'd read. "These people can't swim in their ocean or eat their fish. Because of disease." Caused by waste, human waste, the teacher would delicately explain.

Hey, guess what? Our own nest is pretty foul. And the cause is the birds sitting in it. Us. Every summer, beaches close as soon as there's a big rain and the runoff shoves up the fecal count. More fish die because there's not enough oxygen to go around, thanks to all the algae blooming on all the nitrogen pumped into the water from the sewage treatment plants. More clam flats are closed because the clams are contaminated. A lot of people say you'd be crazy to swim in Nassau County. What with sewer lines overflowing in Hampstead Harbor and that sort of thing.

A little farther east, a man swimming in Huntington Harbor tells me the water's just fine. For now. I call him the migrant swimmer. Because he moves, as the water gets dirtier, during the summer. From Huntington, to Centerport, to Crab Meadow. But most of the young lifeguards at these beaches shake their heads. No, they wouldn't swim here. Not with all the boats. Just common sense not to.

Out where I live, in St. James, the swimming's pretty nice, but the warning signs are there. A Nissequogue man recalls swimming with fifty dolphins in Smithtown Bay.

"And now, I think twice about letting my children eat the fish I catch," Richie L'Hommedieu told a small gathering at Port Jefferson Village Hall last Wednesday. "I don't eat flounder anymore. And I only eat young bluefish. I catch a lot of them with fin rot. And I hardly ever saw a sick fish as a kid."

It was the fourteenth of fifteen citizens' hearings held by the National Audubon Society about the condition of Long Island Sound, which is sick, only most of us are denying how sick. There weren't many people at the meeting. Where was everybody? L'Hommedieu asked. A lot more people use the boat ramp in an hour, he said, than were in this hall.

"The Sound cannot speak for itself," said David Miller, regional vice president of the Audubon Society, urging us to speak for it.

But I think the Sound is speaking, loud and clear, and most of us aren't listening. What could be louder and clearer than this story? The family who told Miller, at a hearing in Connecticut—our neighbors in pollution—of water so pure, they'd take it from the sea to boil their pasta in. Now, when they go out in their boat, they use the oars to push the dead fish away.

I'd taken a swim that very evening, walking down to the water along my favorite path, which is laden with beach roses, the kind that still make you swoon when you stick your nose in them. The sand was cool to my bare feet, as I skirted the poison ivy, a small price to pay for a little wildness. I like walking barefoot in sand, connecting so directly with the earth. It's like holding hands. You get a different sense of the person.

Swimming in salt water is the same thing. We came from the sea. Most of our bodies are salt water, still. So swimming in it is a kind of return. People used to swim in salt water for its healing powers, but now I'd think twice about exposing even a little cut to the Sound.

The Audubon Society's hearings are timed to a five-year federal Long Island Sound Study, which in a year or so will present us with a master plan on how to clean up the mess, and keep it clean. And a big price tag, which is usually the point at which everybody throws up their hands and says, "It's hopeless."

Though we always can find $147 million to build a fourth lane on the LIE, which will encourage more cars and more runoff into the Sound. And we scraped up $4.3 billion, just on the Island, for defense last year. But I don't think it's a question of money so much as imagination. Like the people in Stamford, Connecticut, who cut nitrogen waste by 70 percent by revamping their sewage treatment plant with a biological process that cost $50,000. Hey, that's the cost of a car for some Long Islanders.

We have an attitude problem. We still think America should mean a house and a green lawn for every son and daughter. On land that's already a sodden sponge, full of fertilizers and pesticides. And every time we bulldoze woods and put up condos—like the huge Riviera complex now overlooking Mt. Sinai Harbor—there's less land to absorb the rain water, and more polluted runoff pours into the Sound.

"But you can't tell somebody they can't build a house," says my friend, who owns a construction company. Well, look at the alternative. Another island like Manhattan, where the only bodies swimming in the East River are dead ones.

Why are we still looking the other way when boat operators dump their raw sewage into the water? We don't defecate in our public parks. Why do we just watch when people stand on a dock and throw their barrels of trash into the water? A scuba diver at the hearing said the bottom of the Sound is filling up with shopping carts and tires.

There's a maliciousness to acts like these. Like pouring crankcase oil down a storm drain. And pouring on the lawn chemicals when you know it's ruining the water table.

It's against the law to walk down Main Street and kill people. But it's still okay to kill the earth. Until fin rot starts showing up on us. And we bloom tumors like the fish. And whole cities come down with dysentery and hepatitis, and cancer from the materials we, for some reason, think we can just keep pouring into the land, and the sea, without having them ever come back to kill us, too.

I Loved You,
Mr. Grey

*T*here's an empty space in my garden this fall as I pull up the last of the scarlet runner beans and put away the tomato cages. My cat, Mr. Grey, has been gone for more than a week now. At first, as I searched the woods and roads for him, I worried that he was suffering somewhere, all alone. Now I'm afraid he's dead.

Mr. Grey always kept me company, crouched on the garden wall, waiting for a careless bird, batting at butterflies, and I loved him there, even though it meant the occasional casualty.

He was my first cat, and when he first chased his prey through the dog door of my house, I was horrified. He enjoyed toying with them, driving them into corners and then feigning disinterest, until they skittered for cover beneath the sofa. Then, running low, he'd go for the neck, and their terrified squeaks weren't easy to hear.

I'd always been a dog person before this cat entered my life. I'd gotten him to keep the mice down, but neither my dog, Molly, nor I took to him at first. He'd jump on Molly's tail or stick his nose in my face. I had trouble sleeping in the morning with a cat on my chest.

But soon Molly was letting him lick her face—and checking out his fur for fleas. The three of us sat on the couch together. We took trips together, riding in my red truck down the New Jersey Turnpike.

"Look at that!" we loved to hear the toll takers and gas station attendants say. "A dog and a cat sitting in a car together."

He earned his keep, too. Especially in the fall, when the field mice head for warm pantries, I'd come downstairs in the mornings to find his latest victim laid out on the rug. Sometimes a whole mouse, sometimes a headless mouse, sometimes nothing but a tail.

In the spring, his menu changed—to baby rabbits and squirrels, chipmunks and voles, baby robins and tiny sparrows. I'd find them while vacuuming behind the bureau or the washing machine, or some other lonely place. I'd carry them out to my porch and heave them, with a little prayer, into the woods. It always made me sad, but I'd decided not to curtail Mr. Grey's wild streak. The birds would have to learn to watch out for him, and if a baby or two fell out of the nest, that was the cruelty of nature.

It's the same cruelty I must face now, having let him come and go as he pleased through Molly's dog door, making a little swish in the night that I listen for now, with less and less hope. He was careful about cars, scurrying off into the brush as soon as he heard one coming, so it's more likely that he tangled with a rat or a raccoon and that his death was violent and painful.

I could have kept him inside and not risked his injury or death, but I don't like litter boxes, and I think animals deserve to live outside. I let my dog come and go as well, and I've always lived in the country, where she could roam the woods and bark at the moon. I'm fortunate to have dog-loving neighbors, so there haven't been any angry phone calls warning of leash laws and such.

My dog and cat and I had been a trio for three years—until Mr. Grey disappeared. And now there are empty spaces all through my day. No more swish of the dog door early in the morning as he'd return from a night prowl with a raucous "mrowwww!" demanding his kibble and a spoonful of canned cat food. No more ecstatic kneading of his paws on my chest. No more wrestling matches between him and Molly.

There's an empty spot at the top of the walk where he always sat awaiting my return at night. Now Molly greets me, alone, and we walk sedately down the path—rather than my following the two of them as they raced each other to the door. Mr. Grey was the eight ball in our lives. He zoomed and scooted and stalked and pounced when Molly and I wanted to say, Just sit still, will you?, but now I'd give anything to feel that scratchy tongue on my bare arm.

It's a lonely process, mourning an animal. When a human dies, there's a burial or a cremation and a ritualized grieving, with people coming to the house bearing peach pies and casseroles and sharing, as best they can, the sense of loss.

With an animal, the grief is more private. A close friend may say: "I'm sorry. My cat died a year ago, and I'd been with him for eighteen years." Which is comforting, knowing they've gone through something similar. But there's a bond between Mr. Grey and me that was ours alone. He was devoted to me, and no one else. He didn't ask for much, just a little food and water and a place at the foot of my bed (though he liked the crook behind my knee, too). Maybe a game now and then of rolling the ball with the bell across the floor, or scratching my finger under a blanket and whispering, "What's that, Mr. Grey? Get 'em!"

There really is something to be said for unconditional love, and nobody gives you that, even Mom. Mr. Grey didn't care if I'd flubbed an assignment at work, or hurt my sister's feelings, or let the dishes pile up in the sink. He never wished that I had a perfect. 10 body or fewer wrinkles or blond hair. He never rolled over at night and said, "You know, I've got to tell you about this thing you keep doing that really bugs me."

Such thoughts never entered his tiny brain, of course. But that simple fact—his constant, uncritical affection, the way he fell asleep with his paw on my arm—was something that gave me the strength to go back to work, apologize to my sister, clean up the kitchen or say, "So what is it that really bugs you?"

And he taught me things that no person could know. He made me look at the world differently, from the jaws of a cat holding a baby bird. He was tuned in to a different value system, which he never questioned. And I respected that.

One of the last times I saw him he was hurrying down the walk toward me, proudly bearing his latest catch. My heart sank, as it always did, when I witnessed his kills.

But just then, perhaps from the excitement of showing off his prize, he loosened his grip, and the bird flew off— surprised and unharmed—into the trees. He was mortified.

I don't think cats and dogs have thoughts, really. Perhaps they have images or the memory of smells passing through their brains. But I know they have feelings. They mope if they're abandoned for a few days. They're angry if they get shut up in the house. They're happy chasing a ball or eating something tasty.

I think Molly misses him, though I don't know if she has an image of his gray-and-white face in her mind. But he was such company for her, especially when I was gone for days at a time, that she must feel his absence. A loneliness that this small animal, so innocent and unthinking, is no longer there in the evenings, washing her head from her ears right down to her nose.

I miss him in an animal way, too. I miss his soft, furry body and his loud purring and his sandpaper tongue. I have to face the probability of his death—but if, by chance, he's still alive, I hope he's happy, licking someone else's face.

There's something else I liked about Mr. Grey and me that I could never say about a human relationship: I was never jealous of him. I never had a vindictive thought about him. I always wished him well.

Pieces of the Puzzle

*I*t's quite exciting looking at celery under a microscope. You can see the vessels of the xylem, which conduct water up from the roots, and the cloudy gray of the phloem, the sieve-like mass of living cells that filter all the food manufactured in the leaves throughout the plant.

I sat there, looking at this simple, efficient piece of plumbing and said "Wow," along with the rest of my botany class. I chomped on a piece of my specimen. The flavor hadn't improved; it still needed peanut butter. But knowing more about the whys and wherefores of its watery, fibrous structure made eating celery a little bit more interesting.

Botany 101 is changing my life. I can't take a fall walk these days without thinking about the chlorophyll in every green leaf. During the summer, when sunlight strikes the leaves, and water is drawn up from the roots, and carbon dioxide is sucked out of the air, chlorophyll is busy making us food and giving us oxygen. Without it, we'd be deader than doornails.

And in the fall, when the days shorten and grow colder, the leaves simply stop producing this life-giving green pigment. They are orchestrating their own death, for the sake of the plant's survival. Before falling off the tree, the leaves send any extra food left up there down—through the phloem—for winter storage in the roots.

That's why the leaves turn yellow and orange. The yellow xanthophyll and the orange and red carotene have been there all along—they've just been obscured by the green chlorophyll.

We'd have yellow and orange leaves any fall, regardless of the weather. But it's the brilliant reds and scarlets that are dependent upon a set of weather conditions as precise and balanced as a Bach fugue.

Donald Wyman explains why in his *Trees for American Gardens*. If we get nice warm fall days, with intense sun, the leaves manufacture a lot of sugar, which helps produce a red pigment called anthocyanin. If these warm days are followed by warm nights, those gorgeous reds are simply sent downward, in the form of sugars, for winter food storage.

But if the nights are chilly, with a temperature falling below 45 degrees, that sugar doesn't move. It's trapped in the leaves—the roots lose out a little, but we get to feast our eyes.

Which brings me to my basic question: Does knowing all this, or any of it, improve a walk in the fall?

I used to answer a resounding no, feeling for sure that facts interfered with aesthetics. But that was back in my Dark Ages. With the dawning of science—and in my mind, it's just a little sliver of light—I not only look more, I see more.

It is a little like Pandora's box. One small piece of knowledge leads to another. And another. Soon you are no longer just carrying around Roger Tory Peterson's *Field Guide to the Birds*, which fits so easily in a back pocket, but the Audubon Society's *Field Guide to North American Trees*, which does not. When you tuck your ten-pound botany book under your arm, you've gone too far. You've now become one of those bespectacled nearsighted individuals who'd rather look at a plant under a microscope than kiss somebody under a scarlet maple.

But a little knowledge scattered along a fall trail can intensify its pleasures.

For instance, there are a lot of brown leaves lying out on my deck right now, having fallen from the tree that stands by my cottage door. A year ago, I would have just seen them as brown leaves. Off a tree. Waiting to be swept up. Now I know these big cinnamon-colored food factories have fallen from a chestnut oak—and their nicely rippled edges look entirely different from those of a pin oak or a white oak. And instead of bagging them, I will add them to my soil factory— the garden compost pile.

Now why, I would have sneered last year, should all these little pieces of knowledge add to the pleasures of fall? Just ego, I would have said, the sort of possession that takes place when you can name something, or spiel off yet another fact.

But now, I see things differently. I think knowing about the natural world has more to do with the desire to belong to it, rather than own it. It's the difference between not being able to tell any of your cousins apart at Thanksgiving dinner— and just knowing in your bones, as you pass the turkey, that Joey's eyes are slate blue and Jimmy's are too close together.

There's the same kind of comfortable pleasure in sitting on a tree stump—and recognizing the bittersweet, honeysuckle, wild grape and asters.

The other day—one of those bright still mornings when the yellow sweet gums look as if the lights have been turned on inside each leaf—I took a walk with my dog, Molly, down to the beach.

I saw the shell of a horseshoe crab and thought of what a friend had just told me: We would have a bridge crossing the Sound if not for the fact that Cold Spring Harbor is one of the crab's last mating grounds. That fact put an end to construction plans, saving this quiet paradise for a little longer.

The same friend showed me the long skinny tracks of a great blue heron. He mentioned, casually, the difference between various ducks out on the water—ducks that looked exactly the same to me. He named another bird fluttering off a dock—just a blur to my eye—and I made a note to remember, then promptly forgot. But that's how such comfortable recognitions work—not by painstaking study, but by the regular, casual encounters that breed familiarity.

Sometimes I take a little notebook on these walks. I'm a terrible artist, but my crude attempts at copying the rough squares of the dogwood's bark, and its droopy red leaves, and its stubby little berries, help me to know it.

My favorite tree is the sugar maple—because I climbed it as a kid. I would no more confuse a sugar maple with a silver maple than my sister from yours—because I sat for so long on a wide branch particularly suitable for reading Nancy Drew.

As I climbed the steep hill from the beach, I thought of all the treasures down below. A huge old piece of driftwood perfect for a bench in the woodland garden I am making. Part

of an old chimney that must have tumbled off the cliff in last year's hurricane: I need bricks for a path.

At the top of the hill, I stopped to catch my breath and to admire the white splash of my neighbor's Montauk daisies: just the accent I needed for my chrysanthemum bed. I wondered if he'd give me a few divisions.

Last year, I thought divisions were done in math class, that Montauk was a highway. Now I see them in my garden.

But more important, I see where my garden leads—down the path and through the woods and across the water, and who knows, to other continents and other forests, where leaves and plants are doing nature's business—and, just as a sideline, really, giving us life.

Corn for the Ages

When the dogwoods have leafed out and the leaves of the shadblow are the size of a squirrel's ear, it's time to plant the corn. It's best to get it in the ground before the moon is full—which was last Saturday, so I'm a little late.

"The leaves are signs that the soil is warm enough to plant, and the gravitational pull of the moon helps the growing of the corn," said Nanepashemet, whose Wampanoag ancestors fished and hunted and farmed along the coast of Massachusetts a thousand years ago.

"Tradition states that the crow brought the first corn and bean from the Creator's cornfield in the Southwest, where the Creator lived," he said. "He brought the corn in one ear and the bean in the other."

I'd called Nanepashemet, who is the director of the Wampanoag Indian Program at Plimouth Plantation in Massachusetts, as well as some Native Americans in the Southwest, to find out how to plant the ancient varieties I had gotten from Seeds of Change, an organic heirloom-seed company in Santa Fe, New Mexico.

I have Black Aztec, which was grown in southern Mexico 2,500 years ago, and Rainbow Inca, a multicolored sweet corn with origins in Peru. When fresh, Black Aztec is white and sweet, but as it dries, it turns purplish black, and its hard kernels can be ground into purple cornmeal. Rainbow Inca is red, yellow and bluish black, and a single ear can have 750 seeds.

Biologists think that corn evolved from a wild grain called teosinte that still grows in the Mexican highlands. Popcorn as old as 6,000 years (like what I had at the movies last week) has been found in caves outside Mexico City. But it took thousands of years before that for teosinte to turn from a grassy plant into the first husked kernels of corn that somebody probably threw into a fire one day and watched pop.

Corn cultivation in the Northeast began about 1,000 years ago, Nanepashemet said. "They received corn by trading seed with people farther south, and they also learned the techniques that had developed thousands of years before in South America."

Years ago, when I gardened on a hill overlooking a tidal estuary in Massachusetts, I planted my corn the way the Wampanoags did, putting a few seeds in a loose, sandy mound about three feet across with a herring buried beneath, because the soil was a bit poor.

When the corn was about a handsbreadth high, I hilled soil about the young stalks and kept them weeded. When they were up about seven inches, I planted scarlet runner beans right at the base of the stalks. Then I planted acorn squash at the edge of the mounds—which were six feet apart center to center—and let the vines ramble along the ground. The squash plants kept the soil moist and the weeds down.

The first corn growers in Mexico planted beans next to the corn, without knowing that the legumes were working to help the nitrogen in the soil fertilize the very plants that gave them support. They just copied the combinations they saw growing wild in the highlands.

"It's just how the plants grew in nature," said Alan Kapuler, a microbiologist who searches for heirloom seeds and grows them for his research company, Peace Seeds, in Corvallis, Oregon. "Mexico is the origin of corn, as well as some of the squashes and beans, and you find them growing wild together."

Eaten together, these "three sisters of life," as many native peoples called them, provide the twenty amino acids necessary for complete protein, Mr. Kapuler said. Of course, no one had a chemistry lab 6,000 years ago—people just ate what was there.

When the Tarahumara plant their corn, they dance and sing to it, said Gabriel Howearth, who cofounded Seeds of Change and heads the growing operations at the company's farm in Gila, New Mexico. His grandmother was part Tarahumara, and Mr. Howearth has lived with Tarahumara farmers in northern Mexico, bringing many of their seeds back to Gila.

"Corn is the center of their culture; it's something bred from heaven," Mr. Howearth said. Dances are centered around its planting and when it comes through the ground. Later, when the corn tassels ripen, maidens make offerings with corn pollen.

Many varieties need no irrigation except rain, and the seed is planted deep—more than a foot down. The Tarahumara pray for lightning, too, Mr. Howearth said, because electrical storms free up nitrogen ions from the air. Native people observed the phosphorescent light in the atmosphere during storms, when all the plants look greener than usual. "They're sucking nitrogen from the air," Mr. Howearth said.

The Hopi, too, depend on rain to make the corn grow tall on the reservation outside Flagstaff, Arizona. Denise Masayesva's family was planting corn last week—about eight seeds in every fourth footprint left by Ms. Masayesva's grandfather as he ran down the field. Ms. Masayesva works at Native Seeds/Search, a nonprofit organization dedicated to protecting endangered seed.

It was corn that gave the Hopi their identity.

"When we were wandering, we met this man called Masauw, who is the guardian of this land," Ms. Masayesva said. "He told us, 'You can stay here, provided you take care of the land, but it doesn't belong to you or me.'" Then Masauw gave the Hopi four ears of corn and asked them to choose one.

"He said, 'Which one you choose will determine what will happen to your people,'" Ms. Masayesva said. "We chose the short, stubby one, not the pretty one with the nice coloring. Because this is the one that would survive."

Black Aztec and Rainbow Inca are a long way from Silver Queen and Platinum Lady. But as I plant them all this summer, I will think about the connections.

A Test of Love

As a child, I thought grandmothers grew in gardens. They were always out there in their old cardigan sweaters, watering the flowers. They weren't interested in vegetables, perhaps because they'd lost their appetites over the years. (My own grandmother had to be badgered into eating anything other than bunny bread slathered with King's corn syrup.)

Usually they lived alone, because their husbands had died so long ago. Their men were just photographs on the highboy. So their companions were the bright-colored faces of happy zinnias and tall, exuberant hollyhocks.

This year, I began to understand the powerful bond that my old friends—two grandmothers, a few great-aunts, cousins and a tiny piano teacher—shared with the flowers they grew from seed each summer. At the risk of sounding like an old lady before my time, I, too, have grown to love my hollyhocks and zinnias. Not to mention my nicotiana, morning glories and sunflowers.

(I don't remember any sunflowers in the gray-haired gardens. They were probably too monstrous, like great big dogs that older people may have kept in the past but are now fearful of tripping over.)

This love affair began one Saturday morning in early spring when I wandered into my local garden center to buy some broccoli seeds. I'd always been a vegetable person, a practical type who thought of flowers as a form of organic pest control (marigolds by the beans, nasturtiums in the tomato patch and so forth). Flowers, so I thought, were for people close to death.

Well, they say love comes when you least expect it, and there I was mulling over the "extra good side shoots" of Bonanza Hybrid broccoli and the excellent freezing qualities of Green Comet when the large yellow face of a Mammoth sunflower started flirting at me from the Burpee display rack.

Its appeal was not a subtle whisper. It was more like a scream. *Hey! Aren't I just about the best yellow you ever saw in your life? Do you have any idea how tall I get?*

This flower was just my type. You could actually eat its seeds. And it was well over six feet tall. I could wear high heels.

I added sunflowers to my handful of vegetable seed packets and ordered my feet to head directly to the cashier. But my eyes were locked on the flower seed rack—drinking in the alluring beauties pictured on the brightly colored packets: the ruffly petals of the demure hollyhock, the brilliant orange of a zinnia with the amorous name of Torch.

Suddenly I was awash in memories: the bell-clear days of an island where morning glories opened with the sun, the

heady sweet fragrance of nicotiana adrift on a summer's night, a field of sunflowers—once sown by some farmer visited by a romantic whim—that turned each day, in concert, from east to west.

Then it hit me. *I could grow these things.* I stood for a few minutes, savoring that rare, thunderstruck feeling and letting myself flirt back at other temptresses—all the while knowing with the certainty of love which ones were for me.

And so I brought them home—planting the slow growers like Torch in little pots placed beneath the grow light; saving the rip-roaring types like Mammoth for direct seeding when the ground warmed up. From the outset, their progress was disappointingly ho-hum. Their little leaves didn't interest me, and I became enthralled all over again with the cute notched leaves of the broccoli seedlings, the pungent green suckers of the tomatoes. The flower seedlings got about the same treatment as new arrivals at the office. After the first flurry of excitement, they're ignored for old friends—unless they do something interesting.

Well, they didn't for months.

I began to regret the generous space I'd given them in the vegetable garden—the entire east end, as a matter of fact. And as time went on—and these flowers did *nothing*—I rued that first spring day when I'd fallen head over heels. With what? A bunch of scratchy leaves that allowed themselves to be pockmarked by every bug that landed within a mile. Or silly, limp, flat-looking things that hogged valuable space a prolific bush bean could have used twice over. Just my luck to be wooed by a bunch of sterile plants. Or maybe I'd given them so much high-nitrogen fertilizer they'd produce nothing but leaves.

Then, a zinnia opened. Big deal. It was a dirty white that needed a dose of Clorox thrown in with the wash. A couple of vermilion zinnias followed suit. I wasn't particularly fond of that color. It reminded me of velvet-covered love seats with claws on the feet. No wonder old ladies grew them. I began to feel embarrassed. This was not the image I wanted to convey in my new home. I started acting like one of those creeps who brings somebody to a party and then acts as if she detests him. But I couldn't help myself.

Whenever a visitor strolled by the flower bed and said, "What are all these leaves?" I'd drag them over to the Tendercrop beans to admire their bushy foliage, their little white blossoms. I mean, really. If a humble bean plant can produce a flower without even mentioning it, why can't something that stakes its name on sheer beauty come through with its promise?

Put up or shut up. That's life in the garden—where space and time are limited. As in all matters of love, a certain amount of ruthlessness is involved.

Well, this leafy display continued for months. The morning glory vines clambered all over the garden wall with nary a flower bud. The hollyhocks grew at a snail's pace, flaunting their desiccated leaves. And the sunflowers skyrocketed way over our heads before developing buds about the size of dainty little tea saucers. *Hey! You're supposed to be as big as dinner plates!*

They just ignored me.

Then, as if this had all been some kind of love test, a few droopy flowers appeared amid the stupid thumb-shaped leaves of the nicotiana. Not the most gorgeous things in the world, but their perfume was absolutely seductive. I started hanging out in the garden at night—under the moonlight.

Then the hollyhocks began to unfurl. Each new blossom seemed slightly different in hue, ranging from pale peach to rose to a near scarlet, with a tissue-paper delicacy my fingers had to touch.

The morning glories decided to open all at once. One bright morning the wall was Nantucket blue, the bell-shaped luminous flowers as smooth as a silky morning gown. The bees couldn't resist either. Every hollyhock and morning glory seemed to have some delirious yellow jacket drowning itself in pollen.

And then, while Josh was away at ice hockey camp, his sunflower bloomed. My eleven-year-old gardening friend had tended it faithfully all summer, keeping his doubts to himself. And in his absence, from a magnificent height of twelve feet (just as Burpee's had promised!), it gazed down at me with a humorous benevolence. "See?" it seemed to say, "You gotta have faith."

When Josh returned from the fake ice, he craned his neck at the deep yellow face, every bit as gorgeous as its Burpee photograph, and said, "Wow."

Now, as the winds of September blow up with a hint of fall, we worry that the sunflowers may blow down. Though their stems are as sturdy as wrists, they sway dangerously.

I feel a little old myself when I think how the first hard frost will turn this glorious excess to nothing but brown, limp rags. In a veritable instant—in terms of eternity—this clamorous life will be like the photographs on the highboy. A still silent memory. But how lovely that it ever existed at all.

A NOTE ON THE TYPE

This book was set in Janson, a typeface long thought to have been made by the Dutchman Anton Janson, who was a practicing type-founder in Leipzig during the years 1668–1687. However, it has been conclusively demonstrated that these types are actually the work of Nicholas Kis (1650–1702), a Hungarian, who most probably learned his trade from the master Dutch typefounder Dirk Voskens. The type is an excellent example of the influential and sturdy Dutch types that prevailed in England up to the time William Caslon (1692–1766) developed his own incomparable designs from them.

Composed by Creative Graphics, Inc.,
Allentown, Pennsylvania

Printed and bound by Quebecor Printing,
Martinsburg, West Virginia

Designed by Virginia Tan

Illustrated by Sally Mara Sturman